Amazing Facts: The MEGA Book of Amazing Facts (2,000+ amazing facts)

Jenny Kellett

What a wonderful, wild place our world is! Everyday we are learning something new about the place we live, the body we are in or the history of our universe - and there is never a shortage of amazing facts.

We have brought together over 2,000 of the most mind-blowing and interesting facts that will not only entertain you, but inspire you to learn more about the world around you.

Whether you want to become more knowledgeable or simply want to impress your friends with some cool facts, The MEGA Book of Amazing Facts is sure to blow your mind.

So, here goes...

Science, technology and entertainment facts

The speed of light is 186,000 miles/300,000 km per second.

It takes just eight minutes and 17 seconds for light to travel from the surface of the Sun to the Earth.

Every single year, over one million Earthquakes occur across the planet, but most of them are too small to be felt.

When Krakatoa volcano in Indonesia erupted in 1883, the eruption was heard 3,000 miles/4,800 km away in Australia.

Every second, around 100 lightning bolts hit the Earth.

Around 1,000 people are killed by lightning bolts each year.

Natural pearls can be found in eight different configurations: scope, irregular shape, circle, semicircle, pear, oval, drop and button.

Red eye color occurs only with albinism.

Up to 90 per cent of sunlight is reflected by snow. Land that does not have snow on it typically reflects between 10-20 per cent of all UV rays.

Only one per cent of the world's population are ambidextrous. A person is ambidextrous when they have equal ability in both hands.

The heart creates its own electrical pulses. It can beat even outside the body, but on condition that there is an adequate supply of oxygen.

When a baby is conceived, its heart starts beating after four weeks, and does not stop until death.

Researchers have found that most children are born on a Tuesday, with the least births on a Saturday or Sunday.

When you watch satellite television, the signal travels over 21,747 miles/35,000 km from the nearest satellite.

The human brain needs only 1/20 of a second to recognize an image or object.

Jupiter, despite its heavy weight, is the fastest planet in our Solar System. It takes just 10 hours to do a complete rotation.

The strongest artificial sweetener – lugdunum – is nearly 300,000 times sweeter than sugar.

If you throw a fresh egg into a glass of water, it will sink. A rotten egg will float.

Approximately 95 per cent of a snowflake is just air. This is the reason they fall so slowly, at a speed of just 0.6 miles/0.9 km per hour.

The mineral content and structure of human bones is actually very similar to some species of coral in the southern part of the Pacific Ocean.

Greek philosopher, mathematician and astronomer Archytas of Tarentum created the world's first man made aircraft in the 4th century BC. It had the shape of a bird and could fly a distance of 200 meters with a steam powered jet.

Rainbows occur because sunlight undergoes refraction in water droplets of rain or mist hovering in the atmosphere.

Other people hear our voice in a different way we hear it.

Human lips are over one hundred times more sensitive than fingertips. A kiss is able to increase heart rate to over 100 beats per minute.

Vodka is the cleanest drink in the world.

One day on Mars is 24 hours 39 minutes and 35.244 seconds, which is closer to Earth time than any other planet.

The Milky Way galaxy contains between 200 and 400 billions of stars. There are billions of galaxies in the universe. That's a lot of stars!

One spacecraft can take a photo of one million kilometers of the Earth's surface in just 10 minutes. It would take a normal aircraft four years to do the same job.

Taste buds on the human tongue live for 7-10 days, after which they die and are replaced by new ones.

The impressive colored stripes often seen on the walls of quarries, canyons and mountain slopes appear due to rock minerals: copper (red and orange), iron (green and blue), manganese (black), lime (white). The Grand Canyon is a great example of some of these colors.

Scientists have found that during a flight, high noise levels reduce our sensitivity to sweet and savory dishes; food seems to be somewhat crispy.

When our body is resting, blood needs only six seconds to get from the heart to the lungs and back, and just eight seconds to get to the brain and back.

Malt whiskey has more health benefits than red wine as it contains more ellagic acid — an antioxidant that can stop the growth of cancer cells.

There are 206 bones in the adult human body and there are 300 in children.

The common housefly is one of the most dangerous animals in the world. They transmit more diseases than any other animal.

The first virus in plants and animals was found 100 years ago.

Both food mixers and domestic refrigerators were invented 80 years ago.

The first successful cloning of a human embryo happened five years ago.

The shape of the universe is described as vuvuzela.

Light travels 18 million times faster than rain.

The scientific name for a knee cap is 'patella'.

Octopuses have three hearts.

Kangaroos have three vaginas.

The amount of blood produced by the human heart over a lifetime could fill three supertankers.

Time is the most commonly used noun in the English language.

Every day, all the 'tweets' sent out around the world from social media platform Twitter could fill a 10 million page book.

The average person walks the equivalent of three times around the world in a lifetime.

One third of Russians believe that the Sun revolves around the Earth.

Motor neurons are the longest cells in the human body. They can be up to 1.37 metres long.

Over 50 per cent of NASA employees are dyslexic.

Male zebras are called stallions.

Zebras usually travel in herds.

Oil is formed from the remains of planktonic organisms that lived in the oceans millions years ago.

The first book to have a title including 'Metaphysics' was written by philosopher Aristotle.

The thermal conductivity of a diamond is almost six times higher than that of silver or copper.

Around 19 per cent of solar energy is absorbed by the atmosphere; 47 per cent falls to Earth and the rest returns back to space.

About 27 tons of space dust falls to Earth each day.

Neutron stars are the strongest magnets in the universe.

Ganymede, the largest satellite of Jupiter, is larger than Mercury in size.

There is a phenomenon called "thunder baldness." It's a zone of high voltage that occurs after contact with ground lightning.

If you are standing near the equator, you will weigh 150-200 grams less due to the influence of centrifugal forces from the Earth.

Flashes of different colors that are visible when you rub your eyes are called phosphenes.

The drug Cocaine affects electrical activity of the heart and causes a spasm of arteries, which can lead to a heart attack or stroke.

As the heart produces its own electric pulses, it may continue to beat, even when separated from the body.

----

718 degrees Celsius is the temperature of hell, according to scientists who calculated it by comparing quotes from the Bible.

Antidepressants contribute to the elimination of love because of the increase in serotonin it causes.

According to the French Academy of Sciences, modern humanity speaks almost 3,000 languages.

Sweat is odorless. The bad smell of sweat is a result of it coming into contact with bacteria on the skin's surface.

Many supermarkets have fresh bakery departments closer to the entrance, because the smell of fresh bread encourages people to buy more.

The human eye is so sensitive that if a person sits on top of a mountain on a moonless night, they can detect a lighted match at a distance of 80 kilometers.

One day on Mercury is twice as long as a year and is equal to 176 Earth days.

The fifth day of the week in old Germanic tribes was dedicated to the goddess Freya, which is where the English word 'Friday' came from.

If you removed the space in all atoms of the human body, then what is left would be able to fit through the eye of a needle.

According to psychologists, the presence of a person with glasses increases the opinions of others about that person's IQ by 15 points.

Paper bags are no less harmful to the environment than plastic.

Most digestive processes occur in the small intestine, not in the stomach.

The amount of heat a person's body produces each night is enough to boil 33 litres of iced water.

The large arteries in humans can withstand a pressure of 20 atmospheres.

Sublimation indicates a direct transition from the solid to the gaseous state.

Water can freeze in pipelines at +20°C, if methane is present in the water.

---

14 billion cells are already in the brain at the time of a human birth.

The human eye is capable of seeing 10 million colors.

Peas contain more iodine than any other vegetable.

Leukocytes (white blood cells) live for two to four days in humans; whereas erythrocytes (red blood cells) live for between three to four months.

The Earth's liquid core is located 5,150 km from the surface.

Doctors have proven that the success of treatments for physical ailments can increase by 80 per cent, depending on the mental attitude of the patient.

Gastric juice is capable of dissolving coins if they are made of conventional alloy metal.

In Europe, Luxembourg has the highest percentage of mobile phones per capita.

The word hockey has French roots. The name of the game comes from the word hoquet, which means crook.

Around 100,000 years ago along the coast of Hawaii, ocean waves reached heights of up to 300 meters.

The average English speaker uses about 800 words a day.

Seismologists record about 500,000 earthquakes every year.

When glass cracks, the crack propagates at a speed of 5,000 kilometers per hour.

Microphobia is a fear of small things.

Earth is the only place where you can observe a total solar eclipse.

During a lunar eclipse, shadows move along the surface of Earth at a speed of up to 2,000 meters per second.

Mercury is the closest planet to the sun, but is not the hottest.

The largest lunar crater visible from Earth is called Bailey or 'field of death'.

The moon is the only other known natural astrological object ever walked on.

Humans and giraffes both have seven vertebrae bones in the neck.

The active ingredient in most toothpastes is called sodium fluoride. It can be lethal in high doses.

There are no land snakes in New Zealand.

New Zealand is free of heartworm disease and rabies.

Each year Disneyland uses over 5,000 gallons of paint to maintain the clean appearance of the park.

Giraffes can go without water for longer periods of time than a camel.

Many people who read the word yawn or yawning begin to feel the urge to yawn.

The Titanic carried 1,000 loaves of bread, 86,000 pounds of meat, 40,000 eggs and 36,000 apples to feed its passengers and crew on the seven day voyage.

For a butterfly to fly it must have a body temperature of no less than 30 degrees Celsius.

The first game of chess is believed to have originated in northern India.

Odontophobia is a phobia of going to dentist.

Almonds are members of the rose flower family or rosaceae family.

The tallest girl in the world ever recorded was 8 feet 2 inches tall and died at the young age of 17.

The average human with a full head of hair has around 85,000 to 150,000 hairs on their head.

Squirrels forget where about 50% of the nuts they have hidden are.

The first bullet proof vests were invented by women.

Only humans cry because of feelings.

Mohammad is the most common birth name in the world.

It takes about seven minutes for the average person to fall asleep.

You can give change for a dollar in 293 different coin variations.

About 1 in every 2 million people will die by falling out of bed.

Construction on the Notre Dame Cathedral in Paris began in 1015 A.D and took over 400 years to complete. It was completed in 1439 A.D.

If the human stomach doesn't produce a new layer of mucus every two weeks it will totally digest itself.

75% of the world's population wash themselves in the shower from the top to the bottom.

There are 31,557,600 seconds in a year. A leap year has 31,622,400 seconds.

Approximately one fifth of all the publications from Japan are comic books.

Slugs have four noses. What a lot of people call a nose on a slug is actually a breathing pore called a pneumostome.

Four out of five people over 100 years old are women.

It cost about $7 million to build the Titanic, and around $200 million to make the movie about it.

Birth control pills designed for humans will also work for a gorilla.

If you have a deep fear of the number 13, you may have Paraskevidekatriaphobia. It is also called Friggatriskaidekaphobia or Triskaidekaphobia.

The human gut contains about 1 kg of bacteria.

The planet Mars is rich in water ice.

During female orgasm, endorphins are released, which are powerful painkillers.

SPF stands for Sun Protection Factor.

Comets always have irregular shapes.

Genetic factors have a significant impact on IQ.

The planet Venus's atmosphere absorbs all of the heat surrounding it.

Many European advances during the Middle Ages were made possible by the Moorish occupation of Spain.

The Sun is always losing weight.

Every second, the Sun converts about 700 million tons of hydrogen.

In 1905, Albert Einstein wrote his famous Special Theory of Relativity.

Human foetuses are in fact great fans of rock music.

Sirius star is much brighter than the Sun.

In 1950, the Illinois Central Railroad operated 1,166 steam locomotives and 89 diesel locomotives.

On the moon's surface are large dark patches called seas.

Lithium can alter how you think and has been know to cure certain mental illnesses.

Red dwarf giant stars have surface temperatures of 2,500 Celsius.

There are some people who believe that the future development in robotics will cause a large increase in unemployment.

Asteroids are in fact leftovers that originated from a cloud of gas and dust.

If you slowly pour a handful of salt into a totally full glass of water it will not overflow.

One and two are the only numbers where they are the values of the numbers of factors they have.

Photons have zero mass.

Quicksand doesn't directly kill humans.

If the Sun stopped shining suddenly, it would take eight minutes for people on Earth to notice.

Diamonds aren't the rarest gems on Earth.

1,525,000,000 miles of telephone wires are strung across the United States.

----

101 Dalmatians and Peter Pan (Wendy) are the only two Disney cartoons with both parents that are present and don't die during the movie.

111,111,111 x 111,111,111 = 12,345,678,987,654,321

Each day, 12 newborns will be given to the wrong parents.

----

123 million cars are being driven down the USA's highways.

----

160 cars can drive side by side on the Monumental Axis in Brazil, the world's widest road.

166,875,000,000 pieces of mail are delivered each year in the U.S.

27% of U.S. male college students believe life is "A meaningless existential hell."

Five per cent of Canadians don't know the first seven words of the Canadian anthem, but know the first nine of the American anthem.

----

56 million people go to Major League baseball each year.

----

85 million tons of paper are used each year in the U.S.

99% of the solar system's mass is concentrated in the Sun.

A 10-gallon hat barely holds 6 pints.

A company in Taiwan makes dinnerware out of wheat, so you can eat your plate.

A cow produces 200 times more gas a day than a person.

A dime has 118 ridges around the edge.

Dragonflies have a lifespan of 24 hours.

A fully loaded supertanker travelling at normal speed takes at least twenty minutes to stop.

A hard working adult sweats up to 4 gallons per day. Most of the sweat evaporates before a person realizes it's there.

A jellyfish is 95 percent water.

A "jiffy" is an actual unit of time for 1/100th of a second.

A jumbo jet uses 4,000 gallons of fuel to take off.

A male emperor moth can smell a female emperor moth up to seven miles away.

A mole can dig a tunnel 300 feet long in just one night.

A monkey was once tried and convicted for smoking a cigarette in South Bend, Indiana.

A pig's orgasm lasts for 30 minutes.

A pregnant goldfish is called a twit.

A Saudi Arabian woman can get a divorce if her husband doesn't give her coffee.

A shark is the only fish that can blink with both eyes.

A quarter has 119 grooves on its edge.

A shark can detect one part of blood in 100 million parts of water.

A toothpick is the object most often choked on by Americans!

A walla-walla scene is one where extras pretend to be talking in the background -- when they say "walla-walla" it looks like they are actually talking.

A whale's penis is called a dork.

About 3000 years ago, most Egyptians died by the time they were 30.

About 70% of Americans who go to college do it just to make more money.

According to a British law passed in 1845, attempting to commit suicide was a capital offense. Offenders could be hanged for trying.

Actor Tommy Lee Jones and former vice-president Al Gore were freshman roommates at Harvard University.

Al Capone's business card said he was a used furniture dealer.

All 50 states are listed across the top of the Lincoln Memorial on the back of the $5 bill.

All of the clocks in the movie "Pulp Fiction" are stuck on 4:20.

All porcupines float in water.

Almost a quarter of the land area of Los Angeles is taken up by automobiles.

America's first nudist organization was founded in 1929, by 3 men.

Ancient Egyptians slept on pillows made of stone.

An animal epidemic is called an epizootic.

An average person laughs about 15 times a day.

An iguana can stay underwater for 28 minutes.

An ostrich's eye is bigger than its brain.

Armadillos are the only animal besides humans that can get leprosy.

Armadillos have four babies at a time and they are always all the same sex.

Armored knights raised their visors to identify themselves when they rode past their King. This custom has become the modern military salute.

Aztec emperor Montezuma had a nephew, Cuitlahac, whose name meant "plenty of excrement."

Baby robins eat 14 feet of earthworms every day.

Back in the mid to late 1980's, an IBM-compatible computer wasn't considered a hundred percent compatible unless it could run Microsoft's Flight Simulator.

Bank robber John Dillinger played professional baseball.

If Barbie was life size, her measurements would be: 39-23-33.

Bats always turn left when exiting a cave.

Ben and Jerry's send the waste from making ice cream to local pig farmers to use as feed. Pigs love the stuff, except for one flavor: Mint Oreo.

Bird droppings are the chief export of Nauru, an island nation in the Western Pacific.

Blueberry Jelly Bellies were created especially for Ronald Reagan.

Bubble gum contains rubber.

Camel's milk does not curdle.

Camels have three eyelids to protect their eyes from blowing sand.

Canada is an Indian word meaning "Big Village".

Cat's urine glows under a blacklight.

Cats can produce over one hundred vocal sounds, while dogs can only produce about ten.

Charles Lindbergh took only four sandwiches with him on his famous transatlantic flight.

Chewing gum while peeling onions will keep you from crying.

Clans of long ago that wanted to get rid of their unwanted people without killing them used to burn their houses down - hence the expression "to get fired" from a job.

Cleo and Caesar were the early stage names of Cher and Sonny Bono.

Columbia University is the second largest landowner in New York City, after the Catholic Church.

David Prowse was the guy in the Darth Vader suit in Star Wars. He spoke all of Vader's lines, and didn't know that he was going to be dubbed over by James Earl Jones until he saw the screening of the movie.

You can buy coffee-flavoured PEZ.

The opening credits sequence in "Friends", in which the stars dance in a fountain was shot in the Warner Bros parking lot at 4am.

Dolphins sleep with one eye open.

Dr. Samuel A. Mudd was the physician who set the leg of Lincoln's assassin John Wilkes Booth, and whose shame created the expression for ignominy, "his name is Mudd."

Dr. Seuss pronounced "Seuss" such that it rhymed with "rejoice."

"Dreamt" is the only English word that ends in the letters "mt."

Dueling is legal in Paraguay as long as both parties are registered blood donors.

During your lifetime, you'll eat about 60,000 pounds of food, that's the weight of about six elephants.

Einstein couldn't speak fluently when he was nine. His parents thought he might be retarded.

The first kind of pencil was a bunch of graphite sticks held together by string. Then someone decided it would be better to push the graphite into the inside of a hollow wooden stick.

Joseph Reckendorfer was the first person to think of putting a piece of rubber onto the top of a pencil to make it easier to rub out mistakes.

The average lead pencil allows you to write almost 50,000 English words with just one pencil.

The first bicycle, made in 1817 by Baron von Drais, didn't have any pedals.

The first metal bicycle was called the High-Wheel or Penny Farthing. People had a hard time keeping their balance on this type of bicycle.

The first toy balloon, made of vulcanized rubber, was thought of by someone in the J.G.Ingram company in London, England in 1847.

9-pin bowling was invented in Germany during the Medieval ages.

Karl Benz invented the first gas powered car, which had only three wheels. The first car with four wheels was made in France in 1901 by Panhard et LeVassor.

The first pick-up truck in the world was made by Gottlieb Daimler in 1886.

Gottlieb Daimler produced the world's first motorcycle in 1885.

Gottlieb Daimler also built the world's first taxi in 1897.

The first steam powered train - called the Rocket - was invented by Robert Stephenson.

Romans made the first popsicles. They took some ice and added flavour to it, and then licked it.

The Sumerians, who lived in the Middle East, invented the wheel in about 3450 BC. The Sumerians also invented writing.

The Chinese invented the wheelbarrow.

The opposite sides of a dice always add up to seven.

Many scientists believe that the Earth began billions of years ago as a huge ball of swirling dust and gases.

Lightning strikes Earth about 6,000 times per minute.

There are two types of pandas: the Long-tailed Himalayan carnivore that looks like a raccoon and the Giant panda bear that lives in Western China.

There are two types of camels: One is the Arabian camel that lives in Western Asia and Northern Africa and has one hump. The other is the Bactrian camel, which has two humps and lives in Mongolia and Chinese Turkestan.

There are two kinds of elephants: the African that is taller and has larger ears and the Indian that is small and has smaller ears.

The smallest bird in the world is the Hummingbird. It weighs 1oz.

The fastest human swimmer can swim at 6 miles per hour. The fastest mammal - the dolphin - can swim up to 35 miles per hour.

The bird that can fly the fastest is called a White It can fly up to 95 miles per hour.

Did you know fishes talk to each other? Some of them communicate by making noises in their throats by rasping their teeth, others use their swim bladders to make sounds.

The brain of an average adult male weighs 1,375 gm (55 oz). The brain of Russian novelist Turgenev weighed 2021 gm (81 oz), Bismarck's weighed 1807 gm (72 oz), while that of French statesman Gambetta was only 1294 gm (51 oz). Einstein's brain was of average size.

Napoleon's christening name was Italian: Napoleone Buonaparte (OR Bonaparte). He was born on the island of Corsica one year after it became French property.

The the oldest living thing on earth is 12,000 years old. It is the flowering shrubs called creosote bushes in the Mojave Desert.

A crocodile can't move its tongue and cannot chew. Its digestive juices are so strong that it can digest a steel nail.

Money notes are not made from paper, they are made mostly from a special blend of cotton and linen. In 1932, when a shortage of cash occurred in Tenino, Washington, USA, notes were made out of wood for a brief period.

The Grammy Awards were introduced to counter the threat of rock music. In the late 1950s, a group of record executives were alarmed by the explosive success of rock 'n roll, considering it a threat to "quality" music.

Tea is said to have been discovered in 2737 BC by a Chinese emperor when some tea leaves accidentally blew into a pot of boiling water. The tea bag was introduced in 1908 by Thomas Sullivan of New York.

Over the last 150 years the average height of people in industrialised nations has increased 10 cm (about 4 inches). In the 19th century, American men were the tallest in the world, averaging 1,71m (5'6"). Today, the average height for American men is 1,75m (5'7"), compared to 1,77 (5'8") for Swedes, and 1,78 (5'8.5") for the Dutch. The tallest nation in the world is the Watusis of Burundi.

In 1955 the richest woman in the world was Mrs Hetty Green Wilks, who left an estate of $95 million in a will that was found in a tin box with four pieces of soap.
Queen Elizabeth of Britain and Queen Beatrix of the Netherlands count under the 10 wealthiest women in the world.

Joseph Niepce developed the world's first photographic image in 1827. Thomas Edison and W K L Dickson introduced the film camera in 1894. But the first projection of an image on a screen was made by a German priest. In 1646, Athanasius Kircher used a candle or oil lamp to project hand-painted images onto a white screen.

In 1935 a writer named Dudley Nichols refused to accept the Oscar for his movie The Informer because the Writers Guild was on strike against the movie studios.

In 1970 George C. Scott refused the Best Actor Oscar for Patton.

In 1972 Marlon Brando refused the Oscar for his role in The Godfather.

The system of democracy was introduced 2 500 years ago in Athens, Greece. The oldest existing governing body operates in Althing in Iceland. It was established in 930 AD.

A person can live without food for about a month, but only about a week without water. If the amount of water in your body is reduced by just 1%, you'll feel thirsty. If it's reduced by 10%, you'll die.

According to a study by the Economic Research Service, 27% of all food production in Western nations ends up in garbage cans. Yet, 1.2 billion people are underfed - the same number of people who are overweight.

Camels are called "ships of the desert" because of the way they move, not because of their transport capabilities. A Dromedary camel has one hump and a Bactrian camel two humps. The humps are used as fat storage.

Your body is made up of trillions of cells.

Different parts of your body are made of different kinds of cells.

Your brain is like a computer, and controls your entire body from one central place.

Your heart beats about 70 times a minute, and each time it beats, it pumps about about a cupful of blood

----

An adult human heart weighs about 10 ounces and beats over 100,000 times a day.

There are 206 bones in your skeleton.

About half of the bones in the human body are located in the hands and feet.

Your muscles make up about one-half of your body weight.

If you were to remove your skin, it would weigh as much as five pounds.

About 70 per cent of your body weight is water.

Physics includes the study of light, magnets, electricity, forms of energy, sound and mechanics.

Objects and people move and obey three basic laws of motion: inertia, mass and force, action and reaction.

Inertia, the first law of motion, states that objects that are at rest tend to stay at rest unless acted upon by some outside force. e.g. A ball will not move unless someone kicks it.

The second law of motion deals with the mass (the amount of matter in an object) and force (the action on an object).

The third law of motion, action and reaction, states that for every action there is an equal or opposite reaction.

Isaac Newton discovered the laws of motion more than 300 years ago.

About 10 per cent of the world's population is left-handed.

While sleeping, one in eight people snore, and one in ten grind their teeth.

The average person walks the equivalent of twice around the world in a lifetime.

A cat can run about 20 kph (12 mph) as an adult.

A cheetah can run 76 kph (46 mph).

The fastest human beings run only about 30 km h(18 mph).

A cheetah does not roar like a lion — it purrs like a cat (meow).

The original name for the butterfly was 'flutterby'.

Bears whose brown fur is tipped with lighter-colored hairs are called grizzly bears.

The smallest species of bears is called sun or Malayan bears.

Male bears are called boars.

Bears are native to the continents of North America, Asia, Europe, and South America.

Alaskan brown bears, the world's largest meat-eating animals that live on land, can weigh as much as 1,700 pounds (771 kilograms).

The largest frog in the world is called the Goliath frog. Frogs start their lives as 'eggs' often laid in or near fresh water.

Frogs live on all continents except Antarctica.

Frogs belong to a group of animals called amphibians.

No two zebras have stripes that are exactly the same.

Zebras enemies include hyenas, wild dogs, and lions.

There are more than 50 different kinds of kangaroos.

Kangaroos are native to Australia; they don't live in the wild anywhere else in the world.

A group of kangaroos is called a mob.

Young kangaroos are called joeys.

Reindeers can survive in the extreme cold by eating moss. Moss contains a special chemical that helps them to keep a warmer body temperature.

A chameleon's tongue is twice the length of its body.

A chimpanzee can learn to recognize itself in a mirror, but monkeys can't.

A rat can last longer without water than a camel can.

A woodpecker can peck twenty times a second.

A zebra is white with black stripes.

Porpoises and dolphins communicate with each other by squeaking, growling, moaning, and whistling.

Porpoises and dolphins are mammals.

There are about 40 species of porpoises and dolphins.

Most porpoises and dolphins navigate by using "echolocation".

The largest member of the dolphin family is called an orca or killer whale.

The hippopotamus gives birth under water and nurses its young in the river as well. However, the young hippos do come up for air every now and then.

A cow gives nearly 200,000 glasses of milk in her lifetime.

The world's largest rodent is the Capybara.

An Amazon waterhog, which looks similar to a guinea pig, can weigh more than 100 pounds.

The world's smallest mammal is the bumblebee bat of Thailand, weighing less than a penny.

At 188 decibels, the whistle of the blue whale is the loudest sound produced by any animal.

The fastest dog, the greyhound, can reach speeds of up to 41.7 m/ph.

Greyhounds were believed to have existed in ancient Egypt around 6,000 years ago.

A cat sees about six times better than a human at night because of the tapetum lucidum, a layer of extra reflecting cells that absorb light.

A cat uses whiskers to determine if a space is too small to squeeze through. The whiskers act as antennae, helping the animal to judge the precise width of any passage.

A cat will clean itself with its paws and tongue after it has fought with another cat.

The grizzly bear can run as fast as the average horse.

The female lion does more than 90% of the hunting while the male simply prefers to rest.

At birth, a panda is smaller than a mouse and weighs about four ounces.

A crocodile cannot stick its tongue out.

A cat's jaws cannot move sideways.

All polar bears are left handed.

Ants don't sleep.

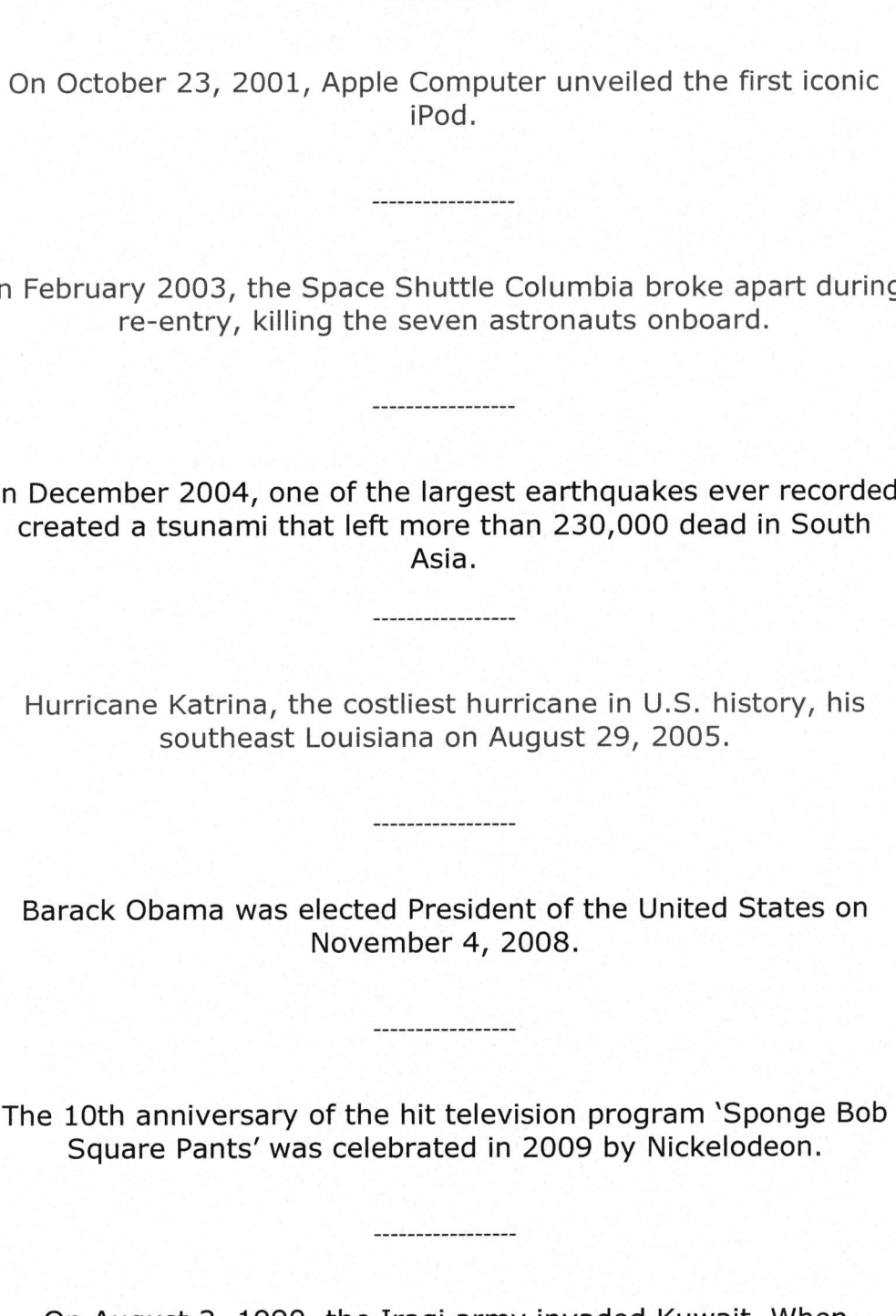

On October 23, 2001, Apple Computer unveiled the first iconic iPod.

In February 2003, the Space Shuttle Columbia broke apart during re-entry, killing the seven astronauts onboard.

In December 2004, one of the largest earthquakes ever recorded created a tsunami that left more than 230,000 dead in South Asia.

Hurricane Katrina, the costliest hurricane in U.S. history, his southeast Louisiana on August 29, 2005.

Barack Obama was elected President of the United States on November 4, 2008.

The 10th anniversary of the hit television program 'Sponge Bob Square Pants' was celebrated in 2009 by Nickelodeon.

On August 2, 1990, the Iraqi army invaded Kuwait. When negotiations failed, the United States-led coalition of military forces attacked the Iraqi Army in January 1991 and officially liberated Kuwait on February 25, 1991.

The first McDonald's restaurant to open in the Soviet Union was in Moscow on January 31, 1991. At the time, it was the largest McDonald's in the world.

A 51-day standoff in Waco, Texas, began when agents from the Bureau of Alcohol, Tobacco, and Firearms attempted to arrest Branch Davidian leader David Koresh on February 28, 1993.

Celine Dion's album *Falling Into You* won the 1996 Album of the Year Grammy Award.

Diana Princess of Wales died in a car accident in Paris, France on August 31, 1997.

John Glenn, at the age of 77, was the oldest astronaut in space when he went up on October 29, 1998.

The Dow Jones Industrial Average closed above 10,000 for the first time on March 29, 1999.

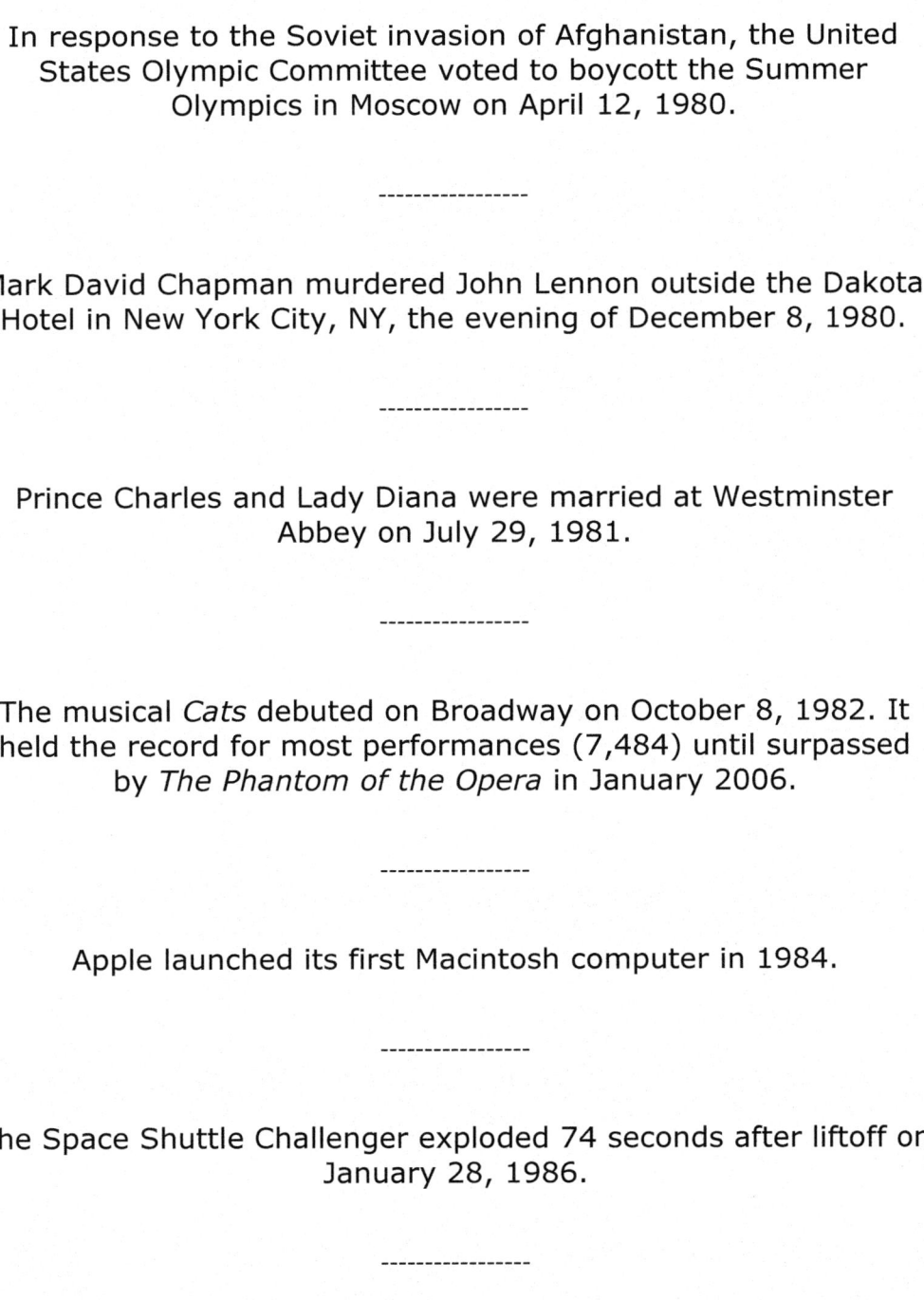

In response to the Soviet invasion of Afghanistan, the United States Olympic Committee voted to boycott the Summer Olympics in Moscow on April 12, 1980.

Mark David Chapman murdered John Lennon outside the Dakota Hotel in New York City, NY, the evening of December 8, 1980.

Prince Charles and Lady Diana were married at Westminster Abbey on July 29, 1981.

The musical *Cats* debuted on Broadway on October 8, 1982. It held the record for most performances (7,484) until surpassed by *The Phantom of the Opera* in January 2006.

Apple launched its first Macintosh computer in 1984.

The Space Shuttle Challenger exploded 74 seconds after liftoff on January 28, 1986.

The stock market lost 22.6 per cent of its value on "Black Monday," October 19, 1987.

A violin is made up of 70 separate pieces of wood.

It took approximately 2.5 million blocks of stone to build the Pyramid of Giza, which is one of the Great Pyramids.

The Sea of Tranquility on the moon is deeper than the highest mountain on Earth.

The first household refrigerator cost about $16,000, in today's money.

A famous bullfighter, Lagartijo, killed 4,867 bulls in the 19th century.

The largest pig on record was a Poland-China hog named Big Bill, who weighed 2,552 lbs.

Carolyn Shoemaker, a famous astronomer, has discovered 32 comets and approximately 300 asteroids.

By recycling just one glass bottle, the amount of energy that is being saved is enough to light a 100 watt bulb for four hours.

In the United States, the first cookbook was published in 1796 and it contained a recipe for watermelon rind pickles.

In a lifetime, the average driver will honk 15,250 times.

Buckingham Palace in London has over six hundred rooms.

Niagara Falls stopped flowing in 1848 for about 20 hours because there was ice blocking the Niagara River.

The colors yellow, red, and orange are used in fast food restaurants because those are the colors that stimulate hunger.

Albert Einstein was offered the presidency of Israel in 1952, but he declined.

A penguin swims at a speed of approximately 15 miles per hour.

A baby octopus is about the size of a flea when it is born.

If all the salt were to be extracted from the Earth's oceans, you would have enough salt to cover all of the continents five feet deep.

The country of Andorra in Europe has a zero percent unemployment rate.

All the Krispy Kreme donut stores collectively could make a doughnut stack as high as the Empire State Building in only two minutes.

In 1685, New France used playing cards as currency because of the shortage of coins.

In North America there are approximately 618 roller coasters.

If someone was to fly once around the surface of the moon, it would be equal to a round trip from New York to London.

Soldier's disease is a term for morphine addiction.

The Civil War produced over 400,000 morphine addicts.

According to scientists, vampire bat saliva is the best known medicine for keeping blood from clotting.

The Colosseum in Rome was used regularly for about 400 years.

Vincent Van Gogh's "Portrait of Dr. Gachet" was the most expensive painting sold at an auction. It was purchased for $85.2 million dollars.

There are about 125 million multiples (twins, triplets, etc.) worldwide.

A squash ball moving at 150 kilometers per hour has the same impact of a .22 bullet.

Your brain is made up of 80% water.

According to a poll, nachos is the food most craved by pregnant women.

The amount of aluminum that Americans throw out in three months is enough to rebuild all American commercial planes.

During World War II, condoms were used to cover rifle barrels from being damaged by salt water as the soldiers swam to shore.

O.J. Simpson had a severe case of rickets and wore leg braces when he was a child.

The material to build the Taj Mahal was brought in from various parts of India by a fleet of 1,000 elephants.

Gardening is said to be one of the best exercises for maintaining healthy bones.

The best time for a person to buy shoes is in the afternoon. This is because the foot tends to swell a bit around this time.

Daytime dramas are called Soap Operas because they were originally used to advertise soap powder.

In America in the early days of TV, advertisers would write stories around the use of their soap powder.

The revenue that is generated from gambling is more than the revenue that comes from movies, cruise ships, recorded music, theme parks, and spectator sports combined.

Angel Falls in Venezuela is the world's highest waterfall, at 979 meters. It is sixteen times the height of Niagara Falls.

There are mirrors on the moon. Astronauts left them so that laser beams could be bounced off of them from Earth. These beams help give us the distance to the moon, give or take a few meters.

There are six million parts in the Boeing 747-400.

At just four years old Mozart was able to learn a piece of music in half an hour.

Bamboo plants can grow up to 36 inches in a day.

Abraham Lincoln's mother died when she drank the milk of a cow that grazed on poisonous snakeroot.

A galactic year is 250 million Earth-years. This is the time it takes for our solar system to make one revolution around the Milky Way galaxy.

Leather skin does not have any smell. The leather smell that you sense is actually from the materials used in the tanning process.

In a year, an average person makes 1,140 phone calls.

The largest ketchup bottle is a 170 feet (52 m) tall water tower.

Russian men who wore a beard during the time of Peter the Great had to pay a special tax.

Morihei Ueshiba, founder of Aikido, once pinned an opponent using only a single finger.

Every three seconds a baby is born somewhere in the world.

The University of Plymouth was the first university to offer a degree in surfing.

In only eight minutes, the Space Shuttle can accelerate to a speed of 27,000 kilometers per hour.

There are more than 40 million Americans that have "chronic halitosis," which is bad breath that never goes away.

It takes about 570 gallons of paint to cover the outside of the U.S. President's home, the White House.

Honolulu, Hawaii boasts the only royal palace in the United States of America.

Central air conditioners use 98% more energy than ceiling fans.

In 1989, 23 people were hired in Jacksonville Florida just to flush toilets so the pipes would not freeze.

By weight, the sun is 70% hydrogen, 28% helium, 1.5% carbon, nitrogen, and oxygen, and 0.5% all other elements.

In the 1985 Boise, Idaho mayoral election, there were four write-in votes for Mr. Potato Head.

One of the steepest main streets in Canada is located in Saint John, New Brunswick. Over a distance of two blocks the street rises about 80 feet.

A Singapore singing group by the name of "The Oriental Singers," sang non-stop for 74 hours and five minutes.

By law, information collected in a U.S. census must remain confidential for 72 years.

Hockey pucks were originally made from frozen cow dung.

Squids move through the ocean using a jet of water forced out of the body by a siphon.

Enough paper is recycled in the USA every day, that a 15 mile long train of boxcars could be filled up with paper.

Someone gets divorced every 10-13 seconds.

People in France own more pets per person than any other country in the world.

There are pink dolphins that live in the Amazon River.

The projection light used for IMAX theaters can be seen from space.

An orca whale can hold its breath for up to 15 minutes.

The Flintstones cartoon was the first 30 minute cartoon to be aired during prime time.

The largest number of children born to one woman, who was a Russian peasant, is 69.

It is believed that shepherds were responsible for inventing the game of golf.

Every day, over five billion gallons of water are flushed down toilets in the United States.

There are about 6,800 languages in the world.

In 1998, a law passed in the U.S. state of Virginia allows drivers to keep their road kill, as long as they report it within 12 hours.

Bill Bowerman, founder of the shoe company Nike, got his first shoe idea after staring at a waffle iron. This gave him the idea of using squared spikes to make the shoes lighter.

Every day, the Hubble telescope transmits enough data to fit 10,000 standard computer disks.

During the 1960's, the women's liberation movement denounced bras as a symbol of servitude and encouraged bra burning rallies.

A one kilogram packet of sugar will have about five million grains of sugar.

In 1819, the USA purchased Florida from Spain for the cancellation of a $5 million debt.

Alaska is the westernmost and easternmost state of the United States. Its islands stretch so far they actually cross the 180th meridian - the global dividing line between "east" and "west".

The three wealthiest families in the world have more assets than the combined wealth of the 48 poorest nations.

In a year, the average person walks four miles to make his or her bed.

A leech has 32 brains.

The longest Hollywood kiss was from the 1941 film, "You're in the Army Now." It lasted for three minutes and three seconds.

The longest engagement on record lasted 67 years, and the couple ended up marrying when they were 82 years old.

The range of a medieval longbow is 220 yards.

Charlie Chaplin once lost a Charlie Chaplin look-alike competition.

John F. Kennedy's rocking chair was auctioned off for $453,500.

According to studies, an average roll of toilet paper lasts about five days in the bathroom.

Ian Fleming's fictional character James Bond made his debut in the 1952 novel "Casino Royale."

On May 9, 1999 approximately 600,000 gallons of whiskey flowed into the Kentucky River during a fire at the Wild Turkey Distillery in Lawrenceburg.

A honey bee strokes its wings about 11,500 times a minute.

Minimum wage was $0.25 per hour when it was first enacted in 1938.

Studies show that couples that smoke during the time of conception have a higher chance of having a girl compared to couples that do not smoke.

In a lifetime, an average man will shave 20,000 times.

Bo Jackson set a Monday Night Football record by rushing for 222 yards in one game against the Seattle Seahawks, including a 91-yard TD run.

The population of the world can live within the state boundaries of Texas.

Honey is the only food that does not spoil. Honey found in the tombs of Egyptian pharaohs has been tasted by archaeologists and was found to be edible.

----

9 out of 10 people believe Thomas Edison invented the light bulb. In fact, Joseph Swan did.

The town of Los Angeles, California, was originally named El Pueblo la Nuestra Senora de Reina de los Ángeles de la Porciúncula.

Washington State has the longest single beach in the USA: Long Beach.

The largest living thing on the face of the Earth is a mushroom underground in Oregon. It measures three and a half miles in diameter.

A German World War II submarine was sunk due to a malfunction of the toilet.

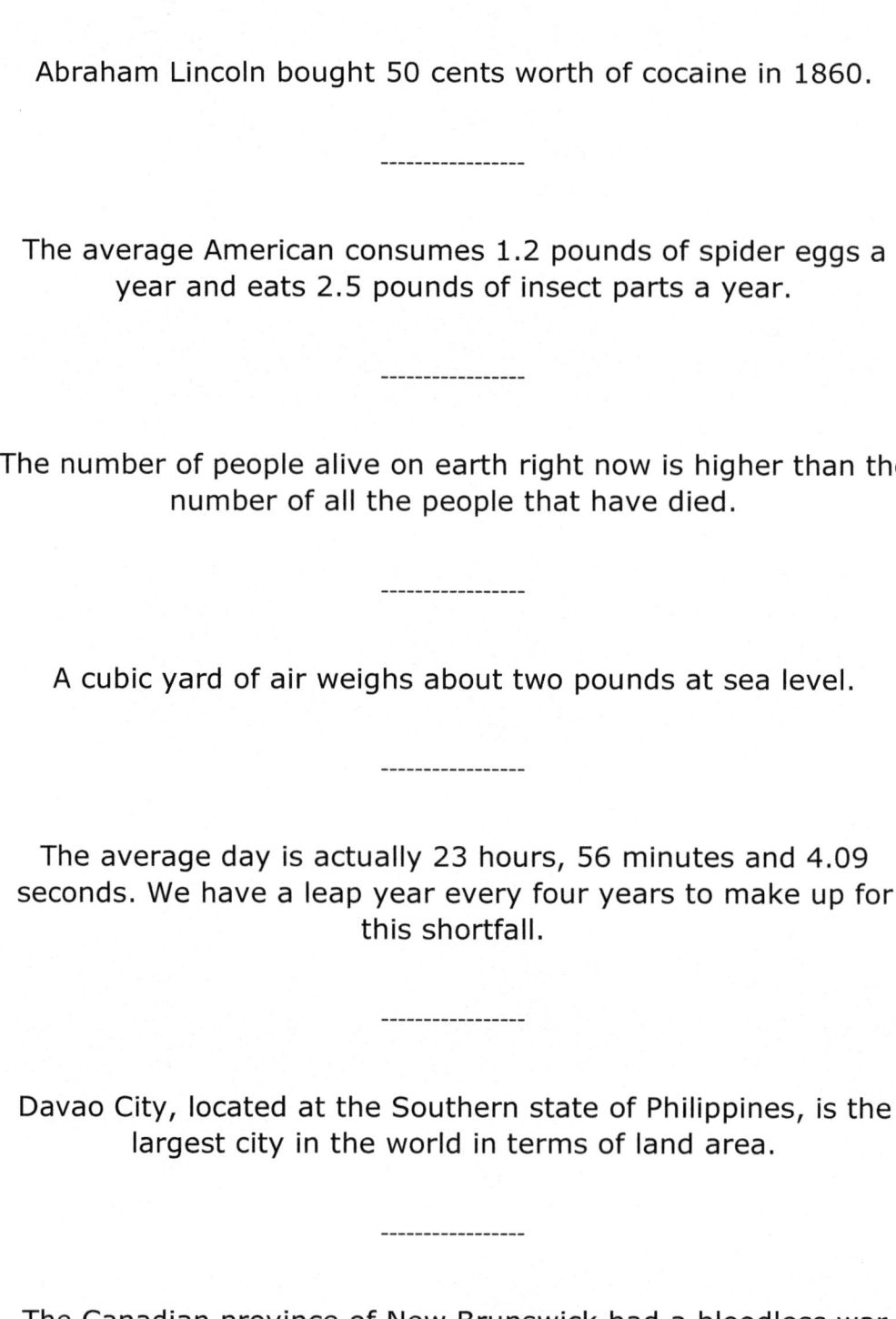

Abraham Lincoln bought 50 cents worth of cocaine in 1860.

The average American consumes 1.2 pounds of spider eggs a year and eats 2.5 pounds of insect parts a year.

The number of people alive on earth right now is higher than the number of all the people that have died.

A cubic yard of air weighs about two pounds at sea level.

The average day is actually 23 hours, 56 minutes and 4.09 seconds. We have a leap year every four years to make up for this shortfall.

Davao City, located at the Southern state of Philippines, is the largest city in the world in terms of land area.

The Canadian province of New Brunswick had a bloodless war with the US state of Maine in 1839.

In Afghanistan, only 25 per cent of the total population has access to clean water.

The United States Forest Service has built more than 360,000 miles of roads in national forests -- or eight times the entire length of the U.S. interstate highway system.

A pig's orgasm lasts up to 30 minutes.

The loudest insect in the world is the male cicadas. When they rub their abdomens, the sound made can be heard from 1300 feet away.

Every U.S. bill regardless of denomination costs 4 cents to make.

There is a substance in the skin of the African clawed frog that helps in fighting infection.

Before air conditioning was invented, white cotton slipcovers were put on furniture to keep the air cool.

The largest diamond found in the United States was a 40.23 carat white diamond. It was found in 1924 and nicknamed the "Uncle Sam."

The largest shopping mall in the world is the West Edmonton Mall located in Edmonton, Alberta, Canada.

American actor Jack Nicholson, and American singer Bobby Darin were raised believing their grandmothers were their mothers and their mothers were their older sisters.

Bill Gates began programming computers at age 13.

The Bible was written by over 40 authors over a period of 1500 years.

Actor Richard Gere was considered to play the role of John McClane in the hit movie Die Hard, but Bruce Willis played the part instead.

Australia has had stamps that actually look like gems. In 1995 and 1996 they used a special technology to make the stamps look like diamonds and opals.

Director George Lucas had trouble getting funding for Star Wars because most studios thought most people wouldn't bother seeing it.

Orville Wright, a pilot, was involved in the first aircraft accident. His passenger, a Frenchman, was killed.

The United States produces enough plastic film annually to cover the entire state of Texas.

The Great Comet of 1843 had a tail that was over 300 kilometers long.

In Israel, religious law forbids picking your nose on Sabbath.

Due to the deforestation of the forests in North China, over one million tons of sands blows into Beijing from the Gobi desert. It sometimes causes the sky to turn yellow.

A leopard's vision is so good it can practically see in the dark.

Centuries ago in India, a person could get their nose chopped off for breaking the law.

Less than 25 per cent of people in the world are vegetarians.

Bernd Eilts, a German artist, turns dried cow manure into wall clocks and small sculptures.

The small intestine in the human body is about two inches around, and 22 feet long.

A piece of French toast that was partially eaten by Justin Timberlake was sold on eBay.

Male goats will pee on each other in order to attract mates.

The word "Oral-B" is a combination of oral hygiene and the letter B, which stands for the word "better."

There is now an ATM at McMurdo Station in Antarctica, which has a winter population of 200 people.

The "Mexican Hat Dance" is the official dance of Mexico.

Singer Michael Jackson owns the rights to the South Carolina State anthem.

An airplane mechanic invented Slinky while he was playing with engine parts and realized the possible secondary use for the springs.

American President Calvin Coolidge (1923-1929) used to like Vaseline being rubbed on his head while he ate breakfast in bed.

Every single hamster in the United States today comes from a single litter captured in Syria in 1930.

The smallest man ever was Gul Mohammed (1957-1997) of India, who measured 1 feet, 10 inches.

The Christmas season begins after sunset on December 24th and lasts until January 5th. This is also known as the Twelve Days of Christmas.

One billion seconds is about 32 years.

Instead of a Birthday Cake, many Russian children are given a Birthday Pie.

In the movie "Babe", the piglet was played by over 30 different piglets, because they outgrew the part so quickly during the production of the film.

The size of a red blood cell is 708 microns. This is equivalent to one millionth of a meter.

Bats can detect food up to 18 feet away.

Tiger Woods is the first athlete to has been named "Sportsman of the Year" by magazine Sports Illustrated two times.

The music for "The Star Spangled Banner" comes from a British drinking song named "Anacreon."

Hershey's has the capacity to wrap up to 1,300 Hershey's Kisses every minute.

There are five million scent receptors located in a human nose.

The artist Michelangelo's full name in Italian is Michelangelo di Lodovico di Leonardo di Buonarroti Simoni.

The oldest documented footwear found was an 8,000 year-old sandal found in a cave located in Missouri, USA.

When the Pez mint dispenser was first introduced it was meant to replace the activity of smoking.

About 500,000 kids in the US live in same sex households.

When a polar bear cub is born, it can not see or hear. It starts to see and hear after about a month.

Over 170,000 Indians from 210 tribes live in the Brazilian Amazon Rainforest.

In 2002, the most popular boat name in the U.S. was Liberty.

When a woman is pregnant, her senses are all heightened.

Elvis Presley had a twin brother named Jesse Garon Presley who died at birth.

The most recycled product in the world is the automobile.

In 1952, Queen Elizabeth II was Time Magazine's "Man of The Year".

Mexico City boasts the world's largest taxi fleet with over 60,000 taxis running every day.

Microsoft made $16,005 in revenue in its first year of operation.

There are approximately 100 million acts of sexual intercourse each day.

India has the most post offices in the world.

Karate originated in India, but was developed further in China.

In November 1999, two women were killed by a lightning bolt
when it hit the underwire in their bras.

In India, a 9-year-old girl was "married" to a stray dog, which tribal custom
requires in order to protect a child whose first tooth appears on the upper gum.

Thirteen per cent of the human population resides in deserts.

The world record for rocking non-stop in a rocking chair is 480
hours held by Dennis Easterling, of Atlanta, Georgia

The average four year-old child asks over 400 questions a day.

The Welwitschia plant can live for up to 1,000 years.

Over 175 million cubic yards of earth was removed for the
creation of the Panama Canal.

Sales of antacids increase by as much as 20 per cent the day after the Super Bowl.

The USS Abraham Lincoln has five gymnasiums on the ship and a basketball league with 22 teams.

A rocket-like device can be traced back to Ancient Greece when a flying steam-powered pigeon was built out of wood.

Studies have shown that surgeons who listen to music while they operate improve in their performance.

Before 1883, the three-cent U.S. stamp was also used for advertising. The advertisement was located on the back of the stamp for various products.

75% of all raisins eaten by people in the United States are eaten at breakfast time.

During the 1600's in England, both boys and girls wore dresses until they were about seven years old.

Steve Fletcher holds the record for the largest gum wrapper collection. His collection has 5,300 gum wrappers from all across the world.

Theodore Roosevelt's mother and first wife died on the same day in 1884.

Serving ice cream on cherry pie was once illegal in Kansas.

No word in the English language rhymes with month, orange, silver or purple.

Maine is the only state whose name is just one syllable.

There are only four words in the English language which end in "-dous": tremendous, horrendous, stupendous, and hazardous.

Tigers have striped skin, not just striped fur.

The characters Bert and Ernie on Sesame Street were named after Bert the cop and Ernie the taxi driver in Frank Capra's "It's a Wonderful Life".

A goldfish has a memory span of three seconds.

It's impossible to sneeze with your eyes open.

John Lennon's first girlfriend was named Thelma Pickles.

Gloucestershire airport in England used to blast Tina Turner songs on its runways to scare birds away.

The name Santa Claus came from Saint Nicholas who was a bishop in the town of Myra, and was known to be very nice to children.

In New York City there are 6,374.6 miles of streets.

Back in 1919, the Russian transplant pioneer Serge Voronoff made headlines by grafting monkey testicles onto human males.

A British term for slot machine is "fruit machine" or "one-armed bandit".

Scientists have determined that having guilty feelings may actually damage your immune system.

Popped popcorn should be stored in the fridge, as this way it can stay crunchy for up to three weeks.

The first modern toothbrush was invented in China. Its bristles came from hogs hair or the mane of a horse that were then put into ivory handles.

Americans did not commonly use forks until after the Civil War.

Actress Jamie Lee Curtis invented a special diaper for babies; that has a pocket.

The first American mention of the Christmas tree was in 1747. However, it was not an actual tree but instead a pyramid made out of wood and decorated with apples and evergreen boughs.

India has a Bill of Rights for cows.

Five thousandths of a millimeter is the tolerance of accuracy at the LEGO mould factories.

A headache and inflammatory pain can be reduced by eating 20 tart cherries.

In 1996, Kermit the frog delivered the commencement address at Southampton College located in the state of New York.

Close to 50 per cent of the bacteria in the mouth live on the surface of our tongue.

The first restaurant to open in Hollywood was the Musso & Frank Grill in 1919.

The drink 7 UP was created in 1929. The original name of the was actually "Bib-Label Lithiated Lemon-Lime Soda".

A poll found that 41% of women apply body or hand moisturizer a minimum of three times each day.

Canadians Scott Abbott and Chris Haney invented Trivial Pursuit. They were planning on playing Scrabble and realized that some of the pieces were missing so they came up with the idea of making their own game: Trivial Pursuit.

The Great Pyramids used to be white because they were encased in a bright limestone that has worn off over the years.

The majority of brides plan their wedding for approximately 7 to 12 months.

An adult lion's roar is so loud that it can be heard up to five miles away.

According to studies, men prefer to have white bedrooms and women prefer to have blue bedrooms.

Singer Paula Abdul used to be a cheerleader for the Los Angeles Lakers.

A language somewhere in the world becomes extinct every two weeks.

A Canadian Tour company offers a two-day course in igloo building.

The first product that the toy company Mattel came out with was picture frames.

The circumference of the African Baobab tree can reach 180 feet. If the trunk is hollow, 20 people would be able to fit inside of it.

In China, people eat a bar of chocolate for every 1,000 chocolate bars eaten by the British.

Babies' eyes do not produce tears until the baby is approximately six to eight weeks old.

The Ice Man, found in the Italian Alps, is now thought to have been murdered. Scientists found an arrowhead stuck in the man's back. He is now known as the oldest murder victim on record.

Scientists at the Texas A&M University's Institute for Biosciences and Technology are working on ways to grow vaccines inside of bananas.

Four per cent of an apple is made up of minerals and vitamins, and over 80% is made up of water.

There is a species of bird, Antpitta avis canis Ridgley, which barks like a dog.

A man named Charles Osborne had the hiccups for around 69 years.

Albert Einstein was cremated and his ashes were spread over a river located in New Jersey.

U-Haul is the world's largest advertiser in the Yellow Pages.

About ten million bacteria live in one gram of soil.

Arabic numerals were not invented by Arabs, but were invented in India by the Hindus.

China is the world's oldest known continuous civilization.

The first subway system in the Americas was built in Boston, Massachusetts in 1897.

The slowest growing finger nail is on the thumb and the fastest growing is the finger nail on the middle finger.

The hog-nosed skunk can spray up to fifteen feet with incredible accuracy.

In 1992, the Antarctic Ozone hole was larger than the continent of North America.

An olive tree can live for up to 1500 years.

An acre of trees can remove about 13 tons of dust and gases every year from the surrounding environment.

Bugs Bunny was originally called "Happy Rabbit".

Construction on the White House began in October of 1792.

In 1983, a Japanese artist, Tadahiko Ogawa, made a copy of the Mona Lisa completely out of ordinary toast.

Romans used to believe that walnuts could cure head problems, since their shape was similar to that of a brain.

The first lighthouse believed to have been built in Alexandria, Egypt in 290 B.C.

According to psychologists, the shoe and the foot are the most common sources of sexual fetishism in Western society.

Corned beef got its name because this beef was preserved with pellets of salt that were the size of corn kernels.

The first company to mass produce teddy bears was the Ideal Toy Company.

Less than 1% of the women in the world will ever be able to wear a diamond that is the size of a carat or more.

Maine is the toothpick capital of the world.

It takes about three hours for food to be broken down in the human stomach.

If you were standing on Mercury, the Sun would appear 2.5 times larger than it appears from Earth.

The turkey was once nominated to be the official bird of the United States.

Even though a red rose may appear to look the same, there are over 900 different types of red roses.

The sound made by the Victoria Falls in Zimbabwe is so loud that it can be heard 40 miles away.

An ear trumpet was used before the hearing aid was invented.

Chanel claims that every 30 seconds, somewhere in the world, a bottle of its perfume Chanel No 5 is sold.

The Taj Mahal was scheduled to be torn down in the 1830's.

The word alligator comes from El Lagarto which is Spanish for the Lizard.

Senior crayon maker, Emerson Moser, retired after making 1.4 billion crayons for Crayola. It was then that he revealed he was actually colorblind.

Thomas Edison, the inventor of the light bulb was afraid of the dark.

After the U.S Civil War, about 33-50% of all U.S paper currency in circulation was counterfeit.

A flea can jump 150 times its size. That is the same as a person able to jump up 1,000 feet in the air.

At lift off, US space shuttles weigh about 4.5 million pounds.

Wal-Mart sells more apparel each year than all the other competing department stores combined.

Approximately 25,000 workers died during the building of the Panama Canal and around 20,000 of them contracted malaria or yellow fever.

It was during World War II that clothes with elastic waists were introduced. This was because the metal used in zippers was needed for the war.

A can of Pepsi has 41 grams of sugar. This amounts to around seven teaspoons of sugar.

The 1960 Summer Olympics were the first Olympic Games to be aired on television by CBS.

Three per cent of pet owners give Valentine's gifts to their pets on Valentine's Day.

Althaiophobia is the fear of marshmallows.

The Nile River is 6,690 kilometers long.

A group of people that are hired to clap at a performance are called a claque.

A South African monkey was once awarded a medal and promoted to the rank of corporal during World War I.

St Patrick, the patron saint of Ireland, was not Irish.

France is known as the perfume capital of the world.

In Alabama, it is against the law to wear a fake mustache that could cause laughter in the church.

44% of kids watch television before they go to sleep.

Blood is such a good stain that Native Americans used it for paint.

When the Statue of Liberty was moved from France to the United States, 214 crates were used to transport it. The Statue was transported in 350 pieces.

Actor Michael Keaton was originally named Michael Douglas.

Marilyn Monroe had six toes.

Artist Vincent Van Gogh sliced part of his ear off in a fit of madness.

The largest volcano known to humans is on Mars: Olympus Mons. It is almost three times higher than Mount Everest.

The most popular ethnic food in the United States is Italian food.

The longest recorded swim was 2938 km down the Mississippi River in 1930. The swimmer spent 742 hours in the water.

On average, men spend 60 hours a year shaving.

The Peregrine Falcon can spot its prey from more than 8 km away.

The chocolate chip cookie was invented in 1933.

Bill Russell was the first black head coach of a major league pro sports team.

The longest recorded duration of a total solar eclipse was seven and a half minutes.

----

215 jeans can be made with one bale of cotton.

The world's largest church is located in Yamoussoukro, the capital of Cote d'Ivoire, Africa.

The act of sneezing is referred to as sternutation.

Consuming chocolate was once considered a sin during the 16th and 17th century.

----

850 peanuts are needed to make an 18 oz. jar of peanut butter.

The lining of a person's stomach is replaced every 36 hours.

Budweiser beer is named after a town in former Czechoslovakia.

The largest school in the world is City Montessori School in India and has over 25,000 students in grade levels ranging from kindergarten to college.

Uranus has 27 moons.

The largest LEGO castle that was ever built was built with 400,000 LEGO bricks.

St. Paul, Minnesota was originally called Pig's Eye after a man named Pierre "Pig's Eye" Parrant who set up the first business there.

In the Netherlands, there are special traffic lanes for bicycles. There are approximately 17,000 kms of cycle lanes with special bicycle traffic lights.

Nintendo was first established in 1889 and they started out making special playing cards.

In 1982, Larry Walters tied 24 weather balloons to his lawn chair in Los Angeles and climbed to an altitude of 16,000 feet.

In China, pancakes are generally served as side dishes. They are stuffed with meat, bean sprouts, and other vegetables.

Americans, on average, use about 580 pounds of paper per year per person.

The word "America" comes from the European explorer "Amerigo Vespucci.

At the equator the Earth spins at about 1,038 miles per hour.

Ancient Egyptians kissed with their noses instead of with their lips.

In a five card poker game there are 2,598,960 possible hands.

The CIA has made a disk camera that is as big as a quarter. This gadget can take many pictures at a time when the disk is opened.

One billion pounds of pasta would need approximately 2,021,452,000 gallons of water to cook it. This is equivalent to 75,000 Olympic-size swimming pools.

In 1958, the United States Coast Guard off western Greenland measured the tallest known iceberg at 550 feet.

In Albania, nodding your head means "no" and shaking your head means "yes."

There are approximately 75 million horses in the world.

A vulture will never attack a human or animal that is moving.

Almonds are the oldest, most widely cultivated and extensively used nuts in the world.

After spending hours working at a computer, look at a blank piece of white paper. It will probably appear pink.

Adult Northwestern American Grizzly Bears can bite through steel as thick as one half inch.

According to Playboy, more women talk dirty during sex than men.

An ant's sense of smell is as good as a dog's.

Americans eat more bananas than any other fruit: a total of 11 billion a year.

An eagle can kill a young deer and fly away with it.

An elephant's trunk contains more than 50,000 muscles.

The adult electric eel can produce a five hundred volt shock, which is enough to stun a horse.

An eyelash lives for about 5 months before falling out.

Americans, on average, eat 18 acres of pizza in one day.

Americans drink over a billion pounds of coffee every year and around five million bottles of soda.

An ear of corn always has an even number of rows because of the genetic formula that divides the cells.

The Library of Congress in Washington, D.C. has the world's largest collection of comic books with over 5,000 titles and 100,000 issues.

The average American drinks 400 glasses of milk in a year.

McDonald's in New Delhi, India makes their burgers with mutton as many Hindus do not eat beef.

The Hawaiian alphabet only has 12 letters.

Benjamin Franklin invented the rocking chair.

Russian I.M. Chisov survived a 21,980ft plunge out of a plane with no parachute. He landed on the steep side of a snow-covered mountain with only a fractured pelvis and slight concussion.

The color blue has a calming effect. It causes the brain to release calming hormones.

One of the terms of Wayne Gretzky's final contract with the New York Rangers was two tickets for every event at New York's Madison Square Garden.

The word Karate means "empty hand."

Since the United Nations was founded in 1945, there have been 140 wars.

The sex of a baby crocodile is determined by the temperature in the nest and how deeply the eggs are buried.

A man filed a lawsuit against his doctor because he survived longer than what the doctor had predicted.

At 120 mph, a Formula One car generates so much down force that it can drive upside down on the roof of a tunnel.

Almost 425,000 hotdogs and buns, and 160,000 hamburgers and cheeseburgers were served at Woodstock '99.

The most valuable painting created by a female artist was "In the Box," painted by Mary Cassatt. It was sold for $3.67 million at Christie's in New York City.

On average, Americans move to a new place eleven times in their lifetime.

Just by recycling one aluminum can, enough energy would be saved to have a TV run for three hours.

Abdul Kassam Ismael, Grand Vizier of Persia in the tenth century, carried his library with him on camels wherever he went.

During the Gold Rush in 1849, some people paid as much as $100 for a glass of water.

In ancient Greece, throwing an apple to a girl was a way to propose for marriage. If the girl caught it, that meant she accepted.

The dromedary camel can drink as much as 100 liters of water in just 10 minutes.

The Shroud of Turin is the single most studied artefact in human history.

Over half the time spent in United States courts is on cases that involve automobiles.

Some of the titles that were considered for the hit television show "Friends" were Six of One, Across the Hall, and Insomnia Cafe.

Iguanas can recognize their human handlers and greet them differently, compared with strangers.

If all the Oreo cookies ever sold were stacked on top of one another, they would be as high as 13.3 million Sears Towers.

Clarence Crane the inventor of "Crane's Peppermint Life Savers" sold his rights to the popular candy for less than $3,000.

Pretzel snacks have been around for over 1300 years.
A monk in Europe invented the snack using used leftover bread dough.

The pound key (#) on the keyboard is called an octothorpe.

Kite flying is a professional sport in Thailand.

Adolf Hitler wanted to be an architect, but he failed the entrance exam at the architectural school in Vienna.

Each year the Pentagon estimates their computer network is hacked about 250,000 times.

From 1939 to 1942, there was an undersea post office in the Bahamas.

7-Eleven is the largest retail chain in the world.

The first commercial microwave oven was called the "1161 Radarange" and was the size of a refrigerator.

The term "mayday" used for signaling for help (after SOS) comes from the French "M'aidez" which is pronounced "MAYDAY" and means, "Help Me."

American Airlines saved $40,000 in 1987 by eliminating one olive from each salad served in first class.

Each day the sun causes about one trillion tons of water to evaporate.

Airports that are at higher altitudes require a longer airstrip due to lower air density.

Frank Wathernam was the last prisoner to leave Alcatraz prison on March 21, 1963.

An average home creates more pollution than the average car does.

An office desk has 400 times more bacteria than a toilet.

Before soccer referees started using whistles in 1878, they used to rely on waving a handkerchief.

New Jersey is referred to as the "Diner Capital of the World" because it has the highest density of diners in the world.

The Titanic's whistles could be heard from 11 miles away.

In Singapore, it is illegal to sell or own chewing gum.

Teflon is the slipperiest substance in the world.

Former U.S. president Ronald Reagan worked as a lifeguard in his youth at a beach near Dixon, Illinois and saved over 77 lives.

Alexandre Gustave Eiffel, the man who designed the Eiffel Tower, also designed the inner structure of the Statue of Liberty.

Actor Bruce Willis's real name is Walter.

The Bank of America was originally called the Bank of Italy until the founder, Amedeo Giannini, changed the name in 1930.

Another word for hiccups is "singultus."

There is a species of kangaroo that is only 2.5 centimeters long when it is born.

Research indicates that people prefer the color blue for their casual clothing.

The six official languages of the United Nations are Arabic, Chinese, English, French, Russian, and Spanish.

According to research, the most productive workday is Tuesday and the least productive is Friday.

18% of an American's income is spent on transportation.

Astronaut Buzz Aldrin's mother's maiden name was "Moon."

Buzz Aldrin was the second man to step onto the Moon in 1969.

Goalies in the National Hockey League played without masks until the year 1959.

The 1912, a wrestling match in Stockholm between Finn Alfred Asikainen and Russian Martin Klein lasted more than 11 hours. Klein eventually won, but was too tired to participate in the championship match.

More than 50% of people in the world have never made or received a telephone call.

The most overdue book in the world was borrowed from Sidney Sussex College in Cambridge, England and was returned 288 years later.

The largest U.S. bill made is for $100,000.

The first American astronaut in space was Alan B. Shepard Jr.

Emilio Marco Palma was the first person born in Antarctica, in 1978.

George Washington grew hemp in his garden.

Halifax, Nova Scotia, Canada has the largest number of bars per capita than anywhere else in the world.

The first domain name ever registered was Symbolics.com.

The most popular name for a pet in the USA is Max.

There was a false floor fitted in Adolf Hitler's Mercedes 770K to make him look taller when he stood up in the car.

Over 500 million gallons of Kool-Aid drink are consumed each year.

Amish people do not believe in the use of aerosol air fresheners.

A 13-year-old boy in India produced winged beetles in his urine after hatching the eggs in his body.

Hawaii's Mount Waialeale is one of the wettest places in the world - it rains throughout the year and receives about 460 inches per annum.

Milk and cheese can aid in the reduction of tooth decay.

A cesium atom in an atomic clock beats over nine billion times a second.

Beijing boasts the world's largest KFC restaurant.

In 1894, the carnival made its debut in North America.

A catfish has about 100,000 taste buds.

There is enough concrete in the Hoover Dam to pave a two lane highway from San Francisco to New York.

On average, a person will spend about five years eating during their lifetime.

Annually 17 tons of gold is used to make wedding rings in the United States.

A blink lasts approximately 0.3 seconds.

The Great Wall stretches for about 4,500 miles across North China.

Oil tycoon, John D. Rockefeller, was the world's first billionaire.

Everyday, U.S. businesses use enough paper to circle the Earth over 20 times.

Every year, Dunkin' Donuts serves an estimated 650 million cups of coffee.

Little Miss Muffet was a girl from the 16th century whose name was actually Patience.

A blue whale's tongue is so large that fifty people could stand on it.

The oldest working Post Office in the world is located in the village of Sanquer, located in the Scottish Lowlands. It has been operating since 1712.

38% of Americans eat breakfast everyday.

The "naked recreation and travel" industry has grown by 233% in the past decade.

Despite being over 27 times smaller, Norway's total coastline is longer than the USA's.

Toronto was the first city in the world with a computerized traffic signal system.

Amtrak is the combination of the words "American" and "Track".

In France, it is illegal for a person to kiss another on railways.

Battle Creek, Michigan is referred to as the "Cereal Bowl of America." The city produces the most breakfast cereals of any city in the world.

Peanut butter is an effective way to remove chewing gum from hair or clothes.

Surfing originated in Hawaii.

The largest hotel in the world is the MGM Grand, which has 5,034 rooms and is located in Las Vegas, Nevada.

Astronauts get taller when they are in space.

Because of its enormous size, the Pentagon operates much like a small city; it has its own shopping mall, power plant, water and sewage facilities, medical clinic, fire station, police force and a mayor.

98% of houses in the United States have at least one television set.

It costs the soft drink industry $100 million a year for thefts committed involving vending machines.

Caterpillar means "hairy cat" in Old French.

An artist from Chicago named Dwight Kalb created a statue of Madonna made out of 180 pounds of ham.

In 1924, Kleenex tissues were originally designed as a cold cream remover.

The cost to build the Empire State Building was $40,948,900.

The Seven Dwarfs are Happy, Grumpy, Dopey, Doc, Bashful, Sneezy and Sleepy.

The first permanent movie theater was the 400-seat Vitascope Hall in New Orleans.

In every episode of Seinfeld there is a Superman character somewhere.

Hang On Sloopy is the official rock song of Ohio.

Speedy Gonzales was fully removed from Cartoon Network due to racial stereotypes until fans–including large Hispanic organizations–demanded he return.

Frank Zappa made a quilt composed entirely of panties that were thrown on stage. He did not wash them first.

The first toilet ever seen on television was on "Leave It to Beaver".

Internationally, Baywatch is the most popular TV show in history.

Carrie Fisher never wore a bra in the first Star Wars movie at the request of George Lucas. He explained to her that in space, her flesh would expand, but her bra wouldn't, so she would be strangled by her bra.

Four people played Darth Vader: David Prowse was his body, James Earl Jones did the voice, Sebastian Shaw was his face and a fourth person did the breathing.

Gilligan of *Gilligan's Island* had a first name that was only used once, on the never-aired pilot show. His first name was Willy.

In Dutch, vader means father.

George Lucas paid the entire $33 million production fee for Star Wars V himself, taking out a loan from the bank. But he made his money back within three months, and the movie became the most successful independent movie of all time.

In 1968, two boys playing in a deserted tenement found the body of a 31yo drug addict, surrounded by religious pamphlets and empty beer bottles. Not until 19 months later was the body identified as that of child actor Bobby Driscoll, Academy Award winner and voice of Peter Pan.

Boris Karloff is the narrator of the seasonal television special "How the Grinch Stole Christmas."

Jackie Chan broke twelve concrete blocks with his hand, while keeping the egg he was holding intact.

Casey Kasem is the voice of Shaggy on "Scooby-Doo."

Cheryl Ladd (of Charlie's Angels fame) played the voice, both talking and singing, of Melody Valentine in the popular 1970's Saturday morning cartoon "Josie and the Pussycats."

Clark Gable used to shower at least four times a day.

Debra Winger was the voice of E.T.

James Doohan, who plays Lt. Commander Montgomery Scott on *Star Trek*, is missing the entire middle finger of his right hand.

Jean-Claude Van Damme was the alien in the original "Predator" movie in almost all of the jumping and climbing scenes.

Legendary Hollywood producer Hal Roach would employ someone called a "wildie" who was either an insane person or a drunk to sit in his writers' room and spout crazy ideas whenever they had writer's block.

Kathleen Turner was the talking voice of Jessica Rabbit, but Amy Irving was her singing voice.

King Kong is the only movie of all time to have its sequel (Son of Kong) released in the same year (1933).

While he was host of "Lorne Greene's Wild Kingdom", Lorne Greene had one of his nipples bitten off by an alligator.

Lynyrd Skynyrd was the name of the gym teacher of the boys who went on to form that band. He once told them, "You boys ain't never gonna amount to nothin'."

Melanie Griffith's mother is actress Tippi Hedren, best known for her lead role in Alfred Hitchcock's *The Birds*.

Of the six men who made up the Three Stooges, three of them were real brothers.

Sharon Stone was the first "Star Search" spokesmodel.

The "Grinch" singer and voice of Tony the Tiger is a man named Thurl Ravenscroft.

The "Whoopi" in Whoopi Goldberg's name came about because she farted all of the time when she was a baby.

The Andy Griffith Show was the first spin-off in TV history. It was spun-off from the Danny Thomas Show.

The band "Duran Duran" got their name from an astronaut in the 1968 Jane Fonda movie "Barbarella."

The famous split-fingered Vulcan salute is actually intended to represent the first letter ("shin," pronounced "sheen") of the word "shalom." As a small boy, Leonard Nimoy observed his rabbi using it in a benediction and never forgot it; eventually he was able to add it to *Star Trek* lore.

The first inter-racial kiss on TV was between Nichelle Nichols and William Shatner in an original *Star Trek* episode entitled *Plato's Stepchildren*.

The first time the word "hell" was spoken on TV was in an original *Star Trek* episode entitled *City on the Edge of Forever*. The quote was "...let's get the hell out of here...", said by William Shatner.

The mask used by Michael Myers in the original "Halloween" movie was actually a Captain Kirk mask painted white.

The name for Oz in *The Wizard of Oz* was thought up when the creator, Frank Baum, looked at his filing cabinet and saw A-N, and O-Z, hence "Oz."

The name of the Vulcan's heaven is Sha Ka Ree, this is a play on the name Sean Connery who was considered for the part of Sarek, Spock's father.

Video Killed the Radio Star was the first video ever played on MTV.

One in every four americans has appeared on television.

Actress Jayne Mansfield accidentally revealed her breast from her dress during the telecast of the Academy Awards in 1957.

During the filming of Lord of the Rings, Sean Bean refused a helicopter ride to the set due to a fear of flying and instead hiked up to it in full Boromir armor.

In the original version of Cinderella the slipper was made out of fur, not glass.

In the movie 'The Wizard Of Oz', Toto the dog's salary was $12 a week, while star of the movie, Judy Garland's was $500 a week.

In Mel Brooks' "Silent Movie", mime Marcel Marceau is the only person who has a speaking role.

Billie Jean by Michael Jackson was the first video to air on MTV by a black artist.

The General Lee cars used in the popular show The Dukes of Hazards were 1969 Dodge Chargers.

The Muppet Show was banned from television in Saudi Arabia because one of its stars was a pig.

The first music video ever played on MTV Europe was Money for Nothing by Dire Straits.

The childhood word game Hangman was the inspiration for television's long-running show Wheel of Fortune.

Kermit the Frog is left-handed and has eleven points on his collar.

A contestant who freezes before the camera on a TV game show is called a "Bambi," in reference to a deer paralyzed by the glare of headlights.

The first letter Vanna White ever turned on the game show Wheel of Fortune was the letter "T."

There were 180 episodes of the sitcom "I Love Lucy".

Lenny Kravitz's mother played the part of Helen on the TV sitcom "The Jeffersons."

Adjusting for inflation, Cleopatra, 1963, is the most expensive movie ever made to date (mid-1999).

After six months at the off-Broadway New York Shakespeare Festival Theater, Hair opened at the Biltmore Theater in New York, in 1968. It was the first rock-musical to play on the Great White Way.

Although largely identified with Scotland, bagpipes were introduced into the British Isles by the Romans.

As of 1996, Hee Haw holds the record for the longest running weekly first-run syndicated show in the history of television. It spanned over 4 decades, from the late 1960s to the early 1990s.

Because of TV censorship, actress Mariette Hartley was not allowed to show her belly button on Gene Roddenberry's Star Trek.

Bette Midler, Barry Manilow and many other famous vocalists got their start in a New York City club called The Continental Baths.

Between 1931 and 1969 Walt Disney collected 35 Oscar awards.

By the time a child finishes elementary school they will have witnessed 8,000 murders and 100,000 acts of violence on television.

C3PO is the first character to speak in Star Wars.

Captain Jean-Luc Picard's fish was named Livingston.

Captain Kirk never said "Beam me up, Scotty," but he did say, "Beam me up, Mr. Scott."

Carnegie Hall in New York City opened in 1891 with Tchaikovsky as the guest conductor.

Chocolate syrup was used for blood in the famous 45 second shower scene in Alfred Hitchcock's movie, *Psycho*, which took seven days to shoot.

Billy Crystal portrayed Jodie Dallas, the first openly gay main character on network television on ABC's Soap, which aired from 1977 to 1981.

Disneyland opened in 1955.

Donald Duck lives at 1313 Webfoot Walk, Duckburg, Calisota.

Donald Duck's middle name is Fauntleroy.

Elvis Presley made his first appearance on national television in 1956. He sang Blue Suede Shoes and Heartbreak Hotel on "The Dorsey Brothers Show."

Despite breaking up 25 years ago, the Beatles continue to sell more records each year than the Rolling Stones.

Gaetano Albert "Guy" Lombardo did the first New Year's Eve broadcast of "Auld Lang Syne," from the Roosevelt Grill in New York City on the eve of 1930.

George Harrison, with "My Sweet Lord," was the first Beatle to have a number one hit single following the group's breakup.

"Happy Birthday" was the first song to be performed in outer space. It was sung by the Apollo IX astronauts on March 8, 1969.

In 1920, 57% of Hollywood movies billed the female star above the leading man. In 1990, only 18% had the leading lady given top billing.

In 1938 Joe Shuster and Jerry Siegel sold all rights to the comic-strip character Superman to their publishers for $130.

In 1962, the Mashed Potato, the Loco-Motion, the Frug, the Monkey, and the Funky Chicken were popular dances.

In 1969, Midnight Cowboy became the first and only X-rated production to win the Academy Award for Best Picture.

In 1987 Playtex premiered the first US TV commercials with real lingerie models displaying their bras and underwear on national television.

In the movie "Casablanca", Humphrey Bogart never said "Play it again, Sam."

In Disney's Fantasia, the Sorcerer's name is Yensid, which is Disney spelled backward.

In October 1959 Elizabeth Taylor became the first Hollywood star to receive $1 million for a single picture. It was for her role in Cleopatra.

In the US, federal law states that children's TV shows may contain only 10 minutes of advertising per hour and on weekends the limit is 10 and one-half minutes.

In the movie, *The Wizard of Oz*, the Scarecrow was looking for a brain, the Cowardly Lion was looking for courage, and the Tin Man was looking for a heart.

Jethro Tull is not the name of the rock singer responsible for such songs as "Aqualung" and "Thick as a Brick." Jethro Tull is the name of the band, and the singer is Ian Anderson.

Jimi Hendrix, Janis Joplin, and Jim Morrison were all 27 years old when they died.

Little Jackie Paper was the name of Puff the Magic Dragon's human friend.

Mickey Mouse is known as 'Topolino' in Italy.

Movie detective Dirty Harry's badge number is 2211.

MTV made its debut at 12:01 a.m. on August 1, 1981.

Napoleon Bonaparte is the historical figure most often portrayed in movies. He has been featured in 194 movies.

On February 9, 1993, "Dateline NBC" was forced to publicly apologize, and NBC president Michael Gartner resigned for a scandal caused by "Dateline" rigging a GM truck with explosives to simulate a scientific crash-test demo.

Penny Marshall was the first female film director to have a film take in more than $100 million at the box office, with her 1988 film "Big".

Pierce Brosnan's first appearance as James Bond was in the 1995 film "Golden Eye".

The beloved Rudolph the Red-Nosed Reindeer, was created in 1939, in Chicago, for the Montgomery Ward department stores as part of a Christmas promotion.

Santa's reindeer are: Dasher, Dancer, Prancer, Vixen, Comet, Cupid, Donner and Blitzen.

The Miss America pageant made its network TV debut on ABC In 1954. Miss California, Lee Ann Meriwether, was crowned the winner.

The first Academy Awards ceremony to be telecast was the 25th, in 1953.

The first Academy Awards were presented in 1927.

The first Grammy Awards were awarded in 1959.

The 1st comic strip was "The Yellow Kid," in the New York World in 1896. The cartoonist was Richard Felton Outcault.

The first feature-length animated film, released by Disney was "Snow White and the Seven Dwarfs" in 1937.

The first ever kiss in a movie was between May Irwin and John Rice in "The Widow Jones," in 1896.

The first live televised murder was in 1963, when Jack Ruby killed John F Kennedy's assassin, Lee Harvey Oswald, while millions of viewers watched.

The first performance of Handel's "Messiah" was on April 13, 1742 at the New Music rooms in Fishamble St., Dublin.

The first televised presidential debate was, between Nixon and Kennedy on September 26, 1960.

The "f-word" was first spoken in a movie by actress Marianne Faithfull in the 1968 film, "I'll Never Forget Whatshisname."

The first winner of the Academy Award for best picture, and the only silent film to achieve that honor, was the 1927 film, "Wings."

The bagpipe was originally made from the whole skin of a dead sheep.

The Beatles' first song to hit the UK charts was 'Love me do' on October 11, 1962.

The Beatles were created in wax at Madame Tussaud's Wax Museum in London, in 1964, the first pop stars to be honored in such a way.

There were two lesser known, previous members of The Beatles: Pete Best and Stu Sutcliffe.

"The Black Hole", released in 1979, was Disney's first PG-rated movie.

For the original Star Wars movie, George Lucas paid a fine and resigned from the Directors Guild rather than obey its demand that he begin with conventional opening credits.

The characters of Homer, Marge, Lisa, and Maggie were given the same first names as The Simpsons creator Matt Groening's real-life father, mother, and two sisters.

The first CD pressed in the US - for commercial release - was Bruce Springsteen's 'Born in the USA'.

The first film granted permission by the Chinese government to be filmed in the Forbidden City was The Last Emperor in 1987.

The first issue of People Magazine, in 1974, cost 35 cents and featured actress Mia Farrow on the cover.

The four main characters from the popular cartoon series "The Chipmunks" are Alvin, Simon, Theodore, and Dave.

"The Jazz Singer", 1927, was the first movie with audible dialogue.

The Lone Ranger's "real" name is John Reid.

The longest Oscar acceptance speech was made by Greer Garson for 1942's "Mrs. Miniver." It lasted 5 minutes and 30 seconds.

The Looney Tunes song has a name. It is called "The Merry-Go-Round Broke Down."

The Mills Brothers have recorded the most songs of any artist: about 2,250.

The Monty Python movie *The Life of Brian* was banned in Scotland.

The official state song of the state of Georgia has been "Georgia on My Mind" since 1922.

The Oscar statuette was designed by MGM's art director, Cedric Gibbons, in 1928. The design has remained unchanged, except for getting a higher pedestal in the 1940's.

The Professor on *Gilligan's Island* was named Roy Hinkley. The Skipper was named Jonas Grumby. Both names were used only once in the entire series -- on the first episode.

The Russian Imperial Necklace has been loaned out by Joseff Jewelers of Hollywood for 1,215 different feature films.

The science-fiction series "Lost in Space" (set in the year 1997) premiered on CBS in 1965.

The song "Happy Birthday to You" was originally written by sisters Mildred and Patty Hill as "Good Morning to You." The words were changed and it was first published in 1935.

The song "When Irish Eyes Are Smiling" was written by George Graff, who was German, and had never visited Ireland.

The term karaoke means "empty orchestra" in Japanese, and the karaoke machine was designed originally to provide backing tracks for solo cabaret performers.

The title role of *Dirty Harry*, 1971, was originally intended for Frank Sinatra.

The Wizard of Oz was a Broadway musical 37 years before the movie version was made.

There have been about 30 films made at or about Alcatraz, the now-closed federal prison island in San Francisco Bay.

Walt Disney's first cartoon character was called Oswald the Rabbit.

Walter Huston and his son John became the first father-and-son team to win Oscars as director of and an actor in "Treasure of Sierra Madre" in 1949.

Saved by the Bell was originally going to have three guys and two girls, but the character of Jesse was created when Elizabeth Berkley had a successful audition.

One of the degrees in Mr. Belding's office on *Saved by the Bell* is for Kung Fu.

On *Saved by the Bell*, Lisa's last name is Turtle, Jessie's middle name is Myrtle, and Zack's pet turtle's name is Myrtle!

In the hit sitcom "Friends", Courteney Cox was originally asked to play Rachel, but she asked to play Monica instead after reading the parts.

Before "Friends" was cast, the main love interest was intended to be Monica and Joey.

Central Perk, the cafe in "Friends" was based on the Manhattan Cafe in New York's West Village. The artwork in there was changed every three episodes.

The first member of the cast of Friends to get a role in a Hollywood film was Marcel the Monkey.

In 1997, The Simpsons broke "The Flintstones" (1960) record for longest-running primetime animated TV show.

Bart Simpson was ranked number one in TV Guide's list of "TV's 10 Biggest Brats".

Homer Simpson works in sector 7-G in the power plant

Bart Simpson's hair has 9 spikes.

The main characters of The Simpsons were given a yellow coloring to attract the attention of channel hoppers.

The Hogwarts motto in Harry Potter, "Draco dormiens nunquam titillandus" means "never tickle a sleeping dragon".

Hugh Grant was originally cast as Gilderoy Lockhart in Harry Potter.

The train station interior used in the film Harry Potter is Kings Cross in North London, whereas the exterior shot is St Pancras.

In the movie, Harry Potter and the Goblet of Fire, full-size models were used in scenes which required actors to keep completely still for long periods.

Emma Thompson accepted the role of Professor Trelawney to impress her four-year-old daughter, Gaia.

A rat's performance in a maze can be improved by playing music written by Mozart.

The real Maria von Trapp makes a brief cameo appearance in the film *The Sound of Music* during the musical number "I Have Confidence."

The song "Happy Birthday" brings in about $2 million in revenue each year for Warner Communications who hold the copyright.

A glockenspiel is a musical instrument that is like a xylophone.

Rapper LL Cool J's name is short for "Ladies Love Cool James."

Yul Brynner was considered for the role of Captain Von Trapp in the film *The Sound of Music*.

Studies have shown that listening to music is good for digestion.

Before he pursued a career in the music industry, Elvis Costello worked as a computer operator at a cosmetics factory.

The biggest disco ball in the world has a diameter of 2.41 meters and weighs 137.89 kilograms.

Gordon Sumner, the rock star and actor known as Sting, got his nickname from the yellow-and-black jerseys he used to wear.

The music band UB40 got its name from an unemployment form in England.

Most cows give more milk when they listen to music.

Natalie Cole, daughter of music legend Nat "King" Cole, became the first black woman to win the Best New Artist Grammy Award.

Aretha Franklin was sued for breach of contract in 1984 when she was unable to open in the Broadway musical "Sing, Mahalia, Sing," because of her phobia of flying.

At 35,000 feet your tastebuds are dramatically decreased meaning that airplane food can taste bland and dull.

The automatic pop up bread toaster was patented before the bread slicing machine.

Ancient Egyptians created jewelry from meteorites by hammering it into shape making beads and other designs.

The world's largest yacht is 590 feet (about 197 yards) long and runs at 94,000 horsepower.

The restaurant 'White Castle' is America's oldest and first hamburger chain.

A Jet Blue flight was grounded and placed out of service after a woman spotted a four inch scorpion between her legs.

Vaejovis Brysoni was the name given to the latest species of scorpion discovered by biologists.

In January of 2013 security officials at O'Hare International airport in Chicago found 18 human heads still covered in skin. They were en route to medical facilities but had errors in the paperwork.

In 1938, Time Magazine chose Adolf Hitler as 'Man of the Year'.

Twelve people have walked on the moon but the last time was in 1972.

Humans and giraffes both have seven vertebrae bones in the neck.

Every month, over 3 million people globally search for something online with the words 'interesting facts' in it, according to Google.

Buttermilk does not contain any butter. It's usually a simple recipe containing lemon juice, white vinegar and milk.

George Washington died on December 14, 1799 at the age of 67. He had ridden his horse around his farm just the day before on a cold, wet day. He awoke the next morning very ill. His last words were "It is well".

The second president of the United States (John Adams) and 3rd president of the United States (Thomas Jefferson) both died within just a few hours apart of each other on the same exact day of July 4th 1826.

Dogs can have a fatal reaction to eating chocolate. Chocolate contains a bitter alkaloid called Theobromine also known as Xantheose, which can be toxic to dogs.

The largest milk producing country by volume in the whole world is India.

In the United States, the Internal Revenue Service has an employee handbook for the collections division unit and in it are instructions that guide employees on how to collect taxes after a nuclear war.

The average human with a full head of hair contains between 85,000 to 150,000 hairs.

Jupiter is the largest planet in the Earth's solar system.

The first bullet proof vest and windshield wiper blades were both invented by women.

Cold weather makes fingernails grow faster.

There are 31,557,600 seconds in a year. A leap year has 31,622,400 seconds.

There is only one metal that's in liquid form at room temperature and that's Mercury.

When water freezes it expands by 10%.

The only animal with four knees is the elephant.

A mid-sized car launched in today's generation generates only an estimated 5 per cent of the pollution that was generated by a car 50 years ago.

A cat's ear has 32 muscles.

The average person laughs 15 times per day.

The eye of an ostrich is larger than it's brain.

A person eats around 60,000 pounds worth of food during their life -- the equivalent of six elephants.

Ants can pull about 30 times their own weight and lift about 50 times their own weight.

A lion can mate more than 50 times in just one day.

Did you know, you cannot fold a 8.5" x 11" or smaller piece of paper in half more than 7 times.

More people are killed from donkeys in a year than on airplanes.

Most snowflakes form with 6 tips or branches. Generally, the colder it is when the snowflake is formed the sharper and more defined the tips will be.

Snails can sleep for up to three years.

If an infant becomes blind soon after they're born they will still almost always see images in their dreams, but infants born with blindness will most likely never have dreams with images.

In the state of Kentucky it was once against the law to carry an ice cream in your back pocket.

On December 16, 1811 the Mississippi river began to flow backwards due to a powerful earthquake.

Fires move much faster uphill than downhill.

Your brain itself can not feel pain.

Researchers say that one week camping without electronics resets our biological body clock and synchronizes our melatonin hormones with sunrise and sunset.

Most people shed between 50 to 100 hairs every day.

The African elephant has a pregnancy that lasts around 22 months - the longest of any mammal.

The Frilled Shark has a gestation period (pregnancy) of up to 3.5 years.

Some sharks lose over 30,000 teeth in a lifetime.

During World War Two, the Oscar awards given out by the American Academy of Motion Picture Arts and Sciences were made of wood because most common metals were scarce.

Breast fed babies score slightly higher on mental development tests than those who are fed on formula.

People who apply sunscreen to themselves generally apply 50-75% less than the recommended amount according to the Archives of Dermatology.

The color of a hens earlobes will usually determine the color of the egg shell.

There are 722 miles of subway track in New York city.

Hartsdale, New York state has a pet cemetery where over 12,000 pets are buried.

Abraham Lincoln died at age 56.

Abraham Lincoln was born on February 12, 1809.

Only one state in the United States contains only one syllable, the state of Maine.

The dog Toto in the movie *The Wizard of Oz's* real name was Terry.

The loudest land animal is the Howler monkey whose deep growls can travel clearly for up to three miles.

The only state in the U.S that grows coffee beans is Hawaii in what's known locally as the Kona district. Hawaiian coffee is some of the most expensive in the world.

England is smaller than the state of Florida by 15,409 square miles.

USGA regulation golf balls have 336 dimples, which add turbulence during flight for more distance.

The lady in the Mona Lisa painting doesn't have eyebrows or eyelashes.

To make one pound of honey, bees would have to visit over two million flowers.

The Oilbird is the loudest bird in the world with it's high pitched clicking sounds.

Soreness after hard work or exercising can be greatly reduced by drinking watermelon juice, according to researchers.

It takes about seven strawberries to equal the amount of vitamin C in one orange about three inches in diameter.

The first food eaten by a U.S astronaut in outer space was applesauce.

The first ever lemon seeds brought to the Americas were by Christopher Columbus.

A Clark's Nutcracker (bird) can store up to 30,000 pine nuts for the winter in over 6,000 different locations across 300 square miles, and remember where at least 70% of them are.

There are more Barbie dolls in Italy than there are Canadians in Canada.

It is physically impossible for pigs to look up into the sky.

If you farted consistently for six years and nine months, enough gas would be produced to create an explosion that is equal to that of an atomic bomb.

If you are attacked by a crocodile, push your thumbs into its eyeballs - it will let go instantly.

In England's parliament, the Speaker of the House is not allowed to speak.

Every continent begins and ends in the same letter.

Every continent in the world has a city called Rome.

Two thirds of the world's eggplants are grown in the state of New Jersey.

The electric chair was invented by a dentist.

Right handed people live on average nine years longer than left handed people do.

The sentence 'the quick brown fox jumps over the lazy dog' uses every letter in the English language.

No president of the United States was an only child.

Typewriter is one of the longest words that can be written using the letters on only one row of a keyboard.

If the population of China walked past you in single file, the line would never end because of the rate of reproduction.

The word racecar and kayak are the same whether they are read left to right or right to left.

China has more English speakers than the United States does.

An average chocolate bar has 8 insects' legs in it.

A cockroach can live nine days without its head before it starves to death.

Donald Duck comics were banned in Finland because Donald Duck does not wear pants.

Stewardesse is one of the longest words typed with only the left hand on a keyboard.

Shakespeare invented the words "assassination" and "bump".

By the age of 65 an average person will have seen 2 million television commercials.

Women blink nearly twice as much as men.

The longest town name in the world has 167 letters. It is in Wales.

A goldfish's attention span is just three seconds.

You burn 20 calories per hour when chewing gum.

An average American will eat 35,000 cookies during their lifetime.

Every day more money is printed for Monopoly than for the US Treasury.

Men can read smaller print than women can; but women can hear better.

Only one out of 1,000 people can lick their elbow.

Most people that read the above fact will try to lick their elbow.

The state with the highest percentage of people who walk to work is Alaska.

The cost of raising a medium sized dog to the age of eleven is $6,400.

The average number of people airborne over the US at any given hour is 61,000.

Intelligent people have been proven to have more zinc and copper in their hair.

The world's youngest parents were eight and nine years old and lived in China in 1910.

The world's youngest pope was 11 years old.

The first novel ever written on a typewriter was Tom Sawyer.

'I am.' is the shortest complete sentence in the English language.

Hershey's Kisses are called that because the machine that makes them looks like it is kissing the conveyor belt.

Babies are born without kneecaps. They do not appear until the child reaches between two to six years of age.

February 1865 is the only month in recorded history not to have a full moon.

In the last 4,000 years, no new animals have been domesticated.

The average American will spend approximately six months waiting at a red light over their lifetime.

On a Canadian two dollar bill, the flag flying over the parliament building is an American flag.

Our eyes are always the same size from birth, but our nose and ears never stop growing.

Peanuts are one of the ingredients in dynamite.

Rubber bands last longer when refrigerated.

An average person's left hand does 56 per cent of the typing.

The Bible does not actually say there were three wise men; it only says there were three gifts.

The cruise liner, QE2, moves only six inches for each gallon of diesel that it burns.

The giant squid has the largest eyes in the world.

The longest word that has one syllable in the English language is 'screeched'.

Microwaves were invented after a researcher walked by a radar tube and a chocolate bar melted in his pocket.

The only word that has 15 letters that can be spelt without repeating a letter is 'uncopyrightable'.

The winter of 1932 was so cold that Niagara Falls froze completely solid.

There are more chickens than people in the world.

Winston Churchill was born in a ladies' room during a dance.

Turtles can breathe through their bottoms.

Dentists have recommended that a toothbrush be kept at least six feet away from a toilet to avoid coming into contact with airborne particles resulting from a toilet flush.

Apples - not caffeine - are more efficient at waking you up in the morning.

Venus is the only planet that rotates clockwise.

The King of Hearts is the only king in a pack of cards without a moustache.

Starfish don't have brains.

Elephants are one of the few mammals that cannot jump.

Catfish have over 27,000 taste buds.

Fleas can jump 350 times their own body length.

Banging your head against a wall burns 150 calories an hour.

The human heart creates enough pressure when it pumps out blood to the body to squirt blood a distance of 30 feet.

If you yelled for 8 years, 7 months and 6 days you would have produced enough sound energy to heat up one cup of coffee.

The dot over the letter 'I' is called a tittle.

Most lipsticks contain fish scales.

A shrimp's heart is in its head.

India's population will overtake China's population in about ten years time.

A man once floated himself into the air using 142 helium filled balloons tied to a lawn chair. He was later arrested for flying without a license.

The world's oldest piece of chewing gum is over 9000 years old.

In space, astronauts cannot cry because there is no gravity, so the tears cannot flow down their faces.

There are more plastic flamingos in the USA than there are real ones.

More people use blue toothbrushes than red ones.

A sneeze travels out your mouth at over 100 miles per hour.

Your ribs move about five million times a year, every time you breathe.

In the White House, there are 13,092 knives, forks and spoons.

Owls are one of the only types of birds who can see the color blue.

An average American or Canadian drinks about 600 cans of soda every year.

It was once against the law to slam your car door in a city in Switzerland.

In Tokyo, a bicycle is faster than a car for most trips of less than 50 minutes.

If you keep a goldfish in a dark room, it will turn white.

Some ribbon worms will eat themselves if they cannot find any food.

The Earth is spinning around the sun at 6,000 miles per hour.

Jupiter has 61 moons.

Human hair and nails keep growing after you die.

There is an official 'The world is flat' club in America with 1,021 members that really believe that is true.

Penguins only live around the South Pole, not the north.

If a cat has blue eyes and white fur by the time it reaches adulthood, there is an 80% chance it will become deaf.

Every day 20 banks are robbed. The average take is around $2500.

One car out of every 230 made was stolen last year.

Almost half of the newspapers in the world are published in the USA and Canada.

There are over 58 million dogs in the US.

Dogs and cats consume over $11 billion worth of pet food a year.

Fingernails grow nearly 4 times faster than toenails.

Humans blink over 10 million times a year.

Every second, Americans collectively eat one hundred pounds of chocolate.

There are approximately 50 copies of the Bibles sold each minute across the world.

Every year, kids in North America spend close to half a billion dollars on chewing gum.

More money is spent on gardening than on any other hobby.

In England in the 1880's, the word 'pants' was considered a dirty word.

Men are six times more likely to be struck by lightning than women.

Of all the words in the English language, the word *set* has the most definitions.

Every 45 seconds a house catches on fire in the United States.

The Sun is 330,330 times larger than the earth.

In Kentucky, it is the law that a person must take a bath once a year.

For each human that is alive, there are 10 million ants.

A typical lead pencil can draw a line that is 35 miles long.

Hippopotomonstrosesquippedaliophobia is the fear of long words.

Noel brand Christmas lights feature a label saying 'for indoor and outdoor use only'.

People say an average 4850 words in a 24 hour period.

India and China combined represent around 36.92% of the world's population.

About 40 per cent of McDonald's profits come from the sale of Happy Meals.

----

315 entries in Webster's 1996 Dictionary were misspelled.

Ketchup was sold in the 1830's as a medicine.

There are no clocks in Las Vegas' casinos.

In Chinese, the KFC slogan "finger lickin' good" comes out as "eat your fingers off".

Brains are more active sleeping than watching TV.

Blue is the favorite color of 80 per cent of Americans.

The average person presses the snooze button on their alarm clock three times each morning.

When the moon is directly overhead, you weigh slightly less.

You cannot kill yourself by holding your breath.

Horses cannot vomit.

If you keep your eyes open by force, they can pop out.

Wearing headphones for just an hour will increase the bacteria in your ear by 700 times.

Approximately 23 per cent of all photocopier faults worldwide are caused by people sitting on them and photocopying their rear ends.

Like fingerprints, everyone's tongue print is different.

Only one person in two billion will live to be 116 or older.

Most of the world's pineapples grow in Hawaii.

Scientists say stupid people laugh more than smart people.

Any month that starts on a Sunday will have a Friday the 13th.

If the planet Saturn was to be put in a bathtub, it would float.

If colorings weren't added to Coca-Cola, it would be green.

If you feed a seagull Alka-Seltzer, its stomach will explode.

Every time you lick a stamp, you are consuming 1/10 of a calorie.

Barbie's full name is Barbara Millicent Roberts.

The bubbles in Guinness beer sink to the bottom rather than float to the top like all other beers.

Smelling bananas and/or green apples can help you lose weight.

Termites eat wood twice as fast when listening to heavy metal music.

Russians generally answer the phone by saying 'I'm listening'.

A lump of pure gold the size of a matchbox can be flattened into a sheet the size of a tennis court.

The placement of a donkey's eyes in its heads enables it to see all four of its feet at all times.

If you multiply 526,315,789,473,684,210 with any number you will always find the original number in the result.

The New York phone book had 22 Hitler's before WWII. The phone book now has 0 Hitler's.

The fingerprints of koala bears are virtually indistinguishable from those of humans, so much so that they could be confused at a crime scene.

Bulls are colorblind; therefore will usually charge at a matador's waving cape no matter what color it is - be it red or yellow.

The 'Hundred Years War' lasted 116 years.

After eating, a housefly regurgitates its food and then eats it again.

The largest eggs in the world are laid by a shark.

The magic word 'Abracadabra' was originally intended for the specific purpose of curing hay fever.

Dogs and cats, like humans, are either right or left handed.

Windmills always turn counter clockwise, except for the windmills in Ireland.

The turkey was wrongly named after what was thought to be its country of origin.

It was illegal to sell E.T. dolls in France because there is a law against selling dolls without human faces.

Oak trees do not have acorns until they are 50 years old or older in age.

There is no mention of Adam and Eve eating an apple in the Bible.

Your heart beats over 100,000 times a day.

The slogan on New Hampshire license plates is 'Live Free or Die'. These license plates are manufactured by prisoners in the state prison in Concord.

Flying from London to New York by Concord (now out of service), due to the time zones crossed, you could arrive two hours before you left.

The sloth (a mammal) moves so slowly that green algae can grow undisturbed on its fur.

There are four cars and 11 light posts on the back of a $10 bill.

There are more beetles than any other kind of creature in the world.

Hummingbirds cannot walk.

The Earth weighs around 6,588,000,000,000,000,000,000,000 tons.

Bruce Lee was so fast that they actually had to slow a film down so you could see his moves.

Cigarette lighters were invented before matches.

It is a criminal offence to drive around in a dirty car in Russia.

An average iceberg weighs 20 million tons.

The Boston University Bridge (on Commonwealth Avenue, Boston, Massachusetts) is the only place in the world where a boat can sail under a train driving under a car driving under an airplane.

A hedgehog's heart beats 300 times a minute on average.

Over 2500 left handed people a year are killed due to using products made for right handed people.

If the population of the Earth continued to increase at its present rate indefinitely, by the year 3530 the total mass of human flesh and blood would equal the mass of the Earth.

Earth is the only planet not named after a God.

A hippo can open its mouth wide enough to fit a four foot tall child inside.

Crickets hear through their knees.

There are more nutrients in the cornflake packaging itself than there are in the actual cornflakes.

The screwdriver was invented before the screw.

On an American one dollar bill, there is an owl in the upper left-hand corner of the '1' encased in the 'shield' and a spider hidden in the front upper right hand corner.

Every photograph of an American atomic bomb detonation was taken by Harold Edgerton.

If you counted 24 hours a day, it would take 31,688 years to reach one trillion.

Human teeth are almost as hard as rocks.

The province of Alberta in Canada has been completely free of rats since 1905.

The longest US highway is route 6 starting in Cape Cod, Massachusetts going through 14 states, and ending in Bishop, California.

The most used letter in the English alphabet is 'E'. 'Q' is the least used.

If you are locked in a completely sealed room, you will die of carbon dioxide poisoning before you will die of oxygen deprivation.

A duck's quack doesn't echo.

Human thigh bones are stronger than concrete.

Only female mosquitoes bite.

A species of earthworm in Australia grows up to 10 feet in length.

It is believed that Shakespeare was 46 years old around the time that the King James version of the Bible was written. In Psalms 46, the 46th word from the first word is 'shake' and the 46th word from the last word is 'spear'.

Pogonophobia is the fear of beards.

The launching mechanism of a carrier ship that helps planes to take off could throw a pickup truck over a mile.

A flush toilet exists that dates back to 2000 BC.

There is about 200 times more gold in the world's oceans than has been mined in our entire history.

A hummingbird weighs less than a penny.

In the Andes, time is often measured by how long it takes to smoke a cigarette.

The longest recorded flight of a chicken is 13 seconds.

Some Eskimos have been known to use refrigerators to keep their food from freezing.

Crocodiles swallow stones to help them dive deeper.

Tens of thousands of birds die each year from smashing into windows.

'Rhythm' is the longest English word without vowels.

Astronauts are not allowed to eat beans before they go into space because passing wind in a spacesuit damages them.

Should there be a crash; Prince Charles and Prince William never travel on the same airplane as a precaution.

Your body is creating and killing 15 million red blood cells per second.

One quarter of the bones in your body are in your feet.

America once issued a 5 cent bill.

The world's population has increased by 3.1 billion in the last 40 years.

When you sneeze, all bodily functions stop including your heart.

An average computer user blinks seven times per minute.

Alfred Hitchcock did not have a belly button.

Walt Disney was afraid of mice.

40,000 Americans are injured by toilets every year.

An average cow produces 200,000 glasses of milk in their lifetime.

Most of the world's maple syrup is from Canada.

The first video game in the world was created in 1958.

The plague that existed in England during medieval times actually still exists today. The last time a person died from the plague was in 2005.

In a study of 200,000 ostriches over a period of 80 years, no one reported a case where an ostrich buried its head in the sand.

In your lifetime you produce enough saliva to fill two swimming pools.

Bees have five eyes.

Someone dies every eight seconds as a result of smoking.

The world's smallest spider is the size of a period.

The NFL makes two Super Bowl trophies, incase one is destroyed during the celebration.

You have no sense of smell when you are asleep.

In 1977, a Mexican town had a storm where frogs fell from the sky.

An iceberg produces more heat than a lit match.

The chance of being killed in a motorbike crash is almost 90 per cent.

The chance of being killed in a car crash is 10 per cent.

Sending an entire building through the mail has been illegal in the US since 1916 when a man mailed a 40,000 ton brick house across Utah to avoid high freight rates.

A man once won an art contest despite his painting was displayed upside down.

An average pigeon can memorize 1200 images.

Coke was invented when two people attempted to create a headache medicine.

The fastest fish in the world can travel at 112 kilometers per hour in water.

Beavers can hold their breath for up to 45 minutes.

Giraffes sleep for 20 minutes a day.

There are 8760 hours in a year.

For each cigarette you smoke, you lose seven seconds of your life.

The distance between the Earth and the Moon is lengthened by two centimeters every year. The moon will begin to orbit Venus in several million years.

The color blue makes you hungry.

If the number of cereal packs produced in 24 hours were placed end to end, the line would reach over 200 miles.

Hummingbirds have the ability to fly backwards.

In the year 210AD, a war occurred where an army of 50,000 soldiers defeated an army of 800,000 soldiers.

Ice cream was invented in China, 4000 years ago.

Hot water can freeze faster than cold water.

Apple seeds are poisonous in large doses.

Due to the rotation of the Earth, an object can be thrown further if it is thrown in a westerly direction.

The two people in the world who have the recipe for Coca-Cola are not permitted to travel in a vehicle together incase of a crash.

At least 15 million people around the world are born on the same day as you.

Every 60 seconds, 100 people die and 240 people are born.

A flamingo's skin color is determined by the food that it eats.

Cows can walk upstairs, but cannot walk downstairs.

The Earth is 0.02 degrees hotter during a full moon.

Religion

Researchers believe that there were female priests in Ancient Egypt.

Religious knowledge was not a necessary requirement for entering the priesthood in Ancient Egypt.

Each temple in Ancient Egypt was dedicated to a particular God in Egypt and they were not places of worship for the public. They also served as vast grain banks.

Hindus worship many gods.

Hinduism is the world's oldest known religion.

The History of Hinduism can be traced back to 5000-10,000 B.C.

Most Hindus live in India, Nepal and Sri Lanka. 85 per cent of Hindus live in India, which is why the country is also known as 'Hindustan'.

The word "Hinduism" actually has no real meaning because Hinduism was not founded as a religion.

Christians believe in one God and in the teachings of Jesus Christ.

Christianity developed out of Judaism in the 1st century C.E.

The three major branches of Christianity are Roman Catholicism, Eastern Orthodoxy, and Protestantism, with numerous subcategories within each of these branches.

The sacred text of Christianity is the Bible, including both the Hebrew scriptures (also known as the Old Testament) and the New Testament.

Christianity is the main religion of America, Europe and Australia.

Islam is the world's second largest
religion, with nearly 1.5 billion followers globally.

Today, Islam is the world's fastest growing religion.

The majority of the world's Muslims live in South and Central
Asia, the Middle East and North Africa.

Indonesia has the world's largest Muslim population, followed by
Pakistan, Bangladesh, India, Turkey, Iran, Egypt, Nigeria, China,
and Algeria.

In both India and China, Muslims are large minorities among
other religions.

Like Christianity and Judaism, Islam was founded in the Middle
East.

Islam's message was preached by the Prophet Muhammad in the 7th century as a continuation of the monotheistic tradition taught by Abraham, Moses and Jesus.

Muslims worship the same god that Christians and Jews worship.

According to Islamic belief, Muhammad was God's last prophet and messenger to humanity.

A central principle of the Islamic faith is respect for all religions, based on the belief that humankind universally worships the same God.

The word "Allah" is Arabic for God.

The word Islam comes from "salaam," which literally means "peace".

Islam encourages Muslims to live a life guided by equity, kindness, honesty, charity, reflection, respect and humility.

A Muslim (pronounced muhs-lim) is a person who submits to God and follows the teachings of Islam as found in the Holy Qur'an.

Many people confuse the terms "Muslim" and "Arab," although they have different meanings. A Muslim refers to someone who follows the teachings of Islam. An Arab refers to a person of Arab heritage who speaks Arabic.

Approximately 10 per cent of the Arab world is not Muslim, and the majority of Muslims are not Arab.

Islam was founded by the prophet Muhammad in Arabia in 622 AD.

Muslims neither worship Muhammad nor pray through him. Muslims solely worship the unseen and Omniscient Creator, Allah.

Sikhism was founded in India in the 1400s by Guru Nanak Dev.

The word "Sikh" means "disciple."

A Sikh place of worship is known as the gurdwara. The word gurdwara means "doorway to God".

The Five Ks are the articles of faith that Sikhs wear as ordered by the 10th Guru, Guru Gobind Singh.

Buddhism developed in India from the teachings of Gautama Buddha.

Buddhism is followed by about 300 million people around the world.

The word 'Buddhism' comes from 'budhi', 'to awaken'. It has its origins about 2,500 years ago when Siddhartha Gotama, known as the Buddha, was himself awakened (enlightened) at the age of 35.

Buddhism explains a purpose to life, it explains apparent injustice and inequality around the world, and it provides a code of practice or way of life that leads to true happiness.

Judaism is an ancient "one god" religion that developed in south-west Asia. Its followers are known as Jews.

Judaism was the first major religion to teach the existence of only one god.

The Torah is the primary document of Judaism.

The Torah contains 613 commandments. There are two parts to the Torah: Written Torah and Oral Torah.

Shintoism is the oldest surviving religion of Japan.

Shintoists worship forces of nature, including rocks and trees.

Shinto, the Chinese term for the Japanese Kami no Michi (Way of the Gods), is made up of religious ideas and cults indigenous to Japan.

It is difficult to date the origins of Shinto, but it predated Buddhism, which was introduced to Japan in the sixth century from Korea.

Acts of worship in Shinto consist of prayers, clapping of hands, acts of purification, and offerings.

Shintoism was once a state religion in Japan, but it is now a sect religion, consisting of 13 recognized groups.

Confucianism is based on the teachings of Confucius, a Chinese philosopher born about 580 BC.

Taoism is another Chinese religion. It is based on the teachings of Lao Tzu about 300 BC.

Atheism is the absence of belief in any God, gods or spiritual beings.

Atheists don't use God to explain the existence of the universe, and believe that humans can – and do – establish moral codes to live by without the aid of Gods or scriptures.

Many atheists are also secularists, and are not supportive of any special treatment given by the state to those adhering to an organized religion.

Many Buddhists identify as atheists, as do some adherents of other traditions like Humanistic Judaism and Non-Realism or Christian Atheism.

Agnosticism is the view that the existence or non-existence of God or any deity, and other religious and metaphysical claims, are unknown and/or unknowable.

Non-Religiousness is the lack of religious principles or practices, and being uninvolved with religious matters.

Secularism is primarily based in belief in the separation of church and state.

Most secularists find religious schools problematic.

Secularists support the right of individuals to have a religious faith, and are entirely opposed to discrimination against people because of their religious, or nonreligious, beliefs.

While most secularists are atheists, some are believers in a faith.

Secularists in the UK stress that privileges should not be afforded to religious individuals and entities, and call for, among other things, the elimination of representation of religion in Parliament and the disestablishment of the Church of England.

Folk religion is an umbrella term for local, indigenous practices that are tied to local lifestyles.

A characteristic of some of these folk religions is religious syncretism.

Demographics on Folk Religions are difficult to find and verify due to varied definitions and interpretations of what is, and is not, a folk religion.

There are many branches of Buddhism, including Mahayana Buddhism, Southern or Theravada Buddhism, Eastern or Chinese Buddhism and Northern or Tibetan Buddhism.

Many Buddhists are vegetarians, and believe in reincarnation.

Chinese Folk Religion refers to the local, tribal religious beliefs and practices that have existed in China for thousands of years.

Taoism took shape as a distinct tradition around 550 B.C.E.

Taoism is believed to have been founded by Lao Zi, who wrote the Tao-te-Ching, a key text for Taoist thought.

The "Tao" is generally translated into "the path" or "the way," and refers to a rightful way of living one's life.

Confucianism has no deities or teachings about the afterlife and instead urges individuals to concentrate on doing the right thing in this life.

Many Japanese people don't think of Shinto as a religion, but more as an aspect of Japanese life.

Shinto is often practiced alongside other religions like Buddhism or Confucianism, making the number of its followers difficult to estimate.

Judaism is the earliest of the three monotheistic, Abrahamic religions.

Abrahamic religions trace their origin to Abraham, who is a figure in the Hebrew Bible (Tanakh), New Testament and the Qur'an.

A Jewish temple is called a synagogue.

Many Jews keep a kosher diet.

The Bahá'í Faith was founded in 19th Century Persia after a proclamation of the Báb, who claimed to be a messiah-like figure of Shi'a Islam.

The Báb said there would soon be another in the line of prophets that included Moses, Muhammad and Jesus, and this prophet was Bahá'u'lláh, the founder of the Bahá'í Faith.

Bahá'ís believe that there is one creator deity that has had many prophets.

Bahá'ís consider the spiritual truth of all religions to be the same.

Jainism is a religion based primarily in India, of which a core tenet is that it is an eternal belief system, without beginning or end.

Jains believe that animals and plants, as well as human beings, contain living souls.

Jains are strict vegetarians and live lives that minimize the use of the world's resources.

Like Hindus, Jains believe in reincarnation.

The Druze are a small, monotheistic religious group concentrated primarily in the Eastern Mediterranean.

The Druze believe in one transcendent God that is present in the whole of existence, as opposed to being above existence.

Though it is based on Islam, the Druze faith incorporates beliefs from other philosophies and monotheistic religions.

The Druze do not follow the Five Pillars of Islam, and are therefore not considered part of Islam by many Muslims.

Neo-Paganism refers to a wide variety of modern traditions that emphasize a revival of ancient pagan practices and beliefs.

The largest and most well-known of the neo-pagan religions is Wicca.

Wiccans can be monotheistic - recognizing one God with male and female aspects; polytheistic - believing in many Gods; or atheistic.

One of the primary beliefs of Wicca is the emphasis on equality between the feminine and the masculine.

Many Wiccans are solitary practitioners, while others form groups of believers sometimes referred to as covens or groves.

Wicca is a decentralized religion with individuals developing their own beliefs, rituals and practices.

There are about 34,000 Christian denominations in the world.

The Bible was written in three languages: Hebrew, Aramaic, and Koine Greek.

The Slavonic Orthodox Church has twice as many followers as the Baptist Church.

The 12 disciples were not were not allowed to carry food, money, or extra clothing.

John was the only apostle who witnessed the crucifixion of Jesus.

There are more than 10,000 distinct religious groups in the world.

Dogs are mentioned 14 times in the Bible, lions 55 times, but domestic cats are not mentioned at all.

The Bible is the world's most shoplifted book.

The oldest almost-complete manuscript of the Bible still existing is the Codex Vaticanus, dating from the first half of the 4th century. It is now held in the Vatican library.

The word "Christian" appears only three times in the Bible: Acts 11:26; 26:28; 1 Peter 4:16.

There are 66 books in the Bible, 39 in the Old Testament and 27 in the New Testament.

The 66 books of the Bible is divided into 1,189 chapters consisting of 31,102 verses.

The Old Testament has 929 chapters; the New Testament has 260 (King James version).

The King James Old Testament consist of 592,439 words consisting of 2,728,100 letters; and the New Testament 181,253 words consisting of 838,380 letter (total 3,566,480 letters).

The longest line in the Bible is Esther 8:9 at 89 words, 425 letters.

The longest word in the Bible is Maher-shalal-hash-baz: Isaiah 8:1.

The shortest verse in the Bible is John 11:35: "Jesus wept."

The longest book chapter in the Bible is Psalm 119, the shortest is Psalm 117.

There are 594 chapters before Psalm 117 and 594 chapters after it, making it the center chapter in the Bible.

Malachi, written around 400 BC, is the youngest book in the Old Testament.

St Paul wrote 14 of the 27 books of the New Testament.

The word "Lord" appears 1,855 times in the Bible.

The word "God" appears in every book of the Bible except Esther and Song of Solomon.

The word "grandmother" appears in the Bible only once.

Seven suicides are recorded in the Bible.

In Old Testament times the Mediterranean Sea was called the Great Sea.

The raven is the first bird mentioned in the Bible.

Almonds and pistachios are the only nuts mentioned in the Bible.

Some 200 mosques in Mecca, Islam's holiest city, point the wrong way for prayers.

The only government-authorized ideology in North Korea is Juche, which began in the 1950s.

The word *agnostic* was coined by Thomas Henry Huxley in 1860 – although the agnostic concept is centuries old.

History

The 16th century Escorial palace of King Philip II of Spain had 1,200 doors.

The world's first travel agencies were Cox & Kings, founded in 1758, and Thomas Cook, founded in 1850.

A dog was the first animal in space (that went into orbit). A sheep, duck and rooster were the first animals to fly in a hot air balloon.

Music was sent down a telephone line for the first time in 1876, the same year the phone was invented.

Beer was the first trademarked product. British beer Bass Pale Ale received its trademark in 1876.

Playing cards were known in Persia and India as far back as the 12th century. A pack then consisted of 48 instead of 52 cards.

Excavations from Egyptian tombs dating to 5,000 BC show that ancient Egyptian children played with toy hedgehogs.

Accounts from Holland and Spain suggest that during the 1500s and 1600s, urine was commonly used as a tooth-cleaning agent.

Julius Caesar was the first to encode communications, using what has become known as the Caesar Cipher.

The first ever soap is believed to have been invented in around 2,500 BC. The soap was made of water, alkali and cassia oil.

The first animal in space was the female Samoyed husky named Laika, launched by the Soviets in 1957.

In 1958, the United States sent two mice called Laska and Benjy into space.

In 1961, the United States launched a male chimpanzee named Ham into space.

In 1963, the French launched a cat named Felicette into space.

Great Britain was the first county to issue postage stamps, on 1 May 1840.

As a boy, Napoleon Buonaparte hated the French.

John Rolfe married Pocahontas the Red Indian Princess in 1613.

Only one of the Seven Wonders of the World still survives: the Great Pyramid of Giza.

The first parachute jump from an airplane was made by Captain Berry at St. Louis, Missouri, in 1912.

On 21 June 1913, over Los Angeles, Georgia Broadwick became the first woman to parachute from an airplane.

The first written account of the Loch Ness Monster in Scotland was in 565 AD.

The world's first skyscraper was the 10-storey Home Insurance office, built in Chicago in 1885. However, Romans built buildings at up to eight stories high.

The Romans used to use asbestos in their cloths for daily use – such as dish-towels, napkins, and table cloths.

In Ancient Egypt, the heart was considered to be the center of intelligence – not the brain.

During the plague in the Middle Ages, some doctors wore a primitive form of biohazard suit called "plague suits".

Over the last 3,500 years, it is estimated that the world has had a grand total of 230 years during which no wars took place.

The best selling book of the 15th century was an erotic book called The Tale of the Two Lovers.

In Ancient Egypt, cats were considered sacred. When a family pet cat died, the entire family would shave off their eyebrows and remain in mourning until they had grown back.

The model for Uncle Sam on the famous 1917 post "I want you" is the face of the painter, James Montgomery Flagg. He used his own picture in order to avoid the need to find a model.

There is no such thing as the Congressional Medal of Honor. In 1862, Lincoln signed into law a resolution creating a "Medal of Honor" which is the official and only title for what most people think is the "Congressional Medal".

In 200 BC, when the Greek city of Sparta was at the height of its power there were 20 slaves for every citizen.

Andorra declared war on Germany during World War I, but did not actually take part in the fighting.

Only two people signed the Declaration independence on 4 July 1776 – John Hancock and Charles Thomson. The majority of the other members of Congress signed on 2 August. The final signature wasn't added for another five years.

In ancient Rome, people would drink a mixture of wine and the dung of wild boars, as a restorative medicine.

Sir William Paterson, founder of the Bank of England, is suspected to have been a pirate in his years before founding the iconic bank.

Coca-Cola originally contained cocaine.

Internet was originally called ARPANet (Advanced Research Projects Agency Network). It was designed by the US Department of Defense.

The first Burger King was opened in Miami, Florida in 1954.

Australia was originally called New Holland.

In 1878 the first telephone book made contained only 50 names.

Coca-Cola launched its third product - Sprite - in 1961.

Paper originated in China.

Instant coffee was invented in 1901.

The word 'testify' derived from a time when men were required to swear on their testicles.

Tennis was originally played with bare hands and no racquets.

The Olympic flag was designed in 1913

The electric toothbrush was invented in 1939.

Isaac Newton invented the cat door.

The Titanic was built in Belfast.

Hawaii was originally called the Sandwich Islands.

The doorbell was invented in 1831.

The first English dictionary was written in 1755.

The first city to reach a population of one million people was London.

Tokyo was once known as Edo.

The tea bag was invented in 1908.

Plastic bottles were first used for soft drinks in 1970.

The dollar ($) sign was first introduced in 1788.

The term 'disc jockey' was first used in 1937.

The first ever train reached a top speed of only 8 kph (5 mph).

New York was once called New Amsterdam.

Hawaii officially became a part of the United States in 1900.

New York's Central Park was opened in 1876.

The first rugby club was formed in 1843.

The yo-yo was originally used as a weapon for hunting in the Philippines.

Draughts (checkers) is older than chess.

The first metered taxi was introduced in 1907.

The Chinese used fingerprints as a method of identification as far back as AD 700.

The revolving door was invented in 1888.

Sir Isaac Newton was just 23 when he discovered the law of gravity.

The drinking straw was invented in 1886.

Paper money was first used in China.

Leonardo Da Vinci invented scissors.

All of the cobble stones used to line the streets in New York were originally stones found in the hulls of Belgian ships ballast.

Diet Coke was introduced in 1982.

There is no proof as to who built the Taj Mahal.

In the 17th century the value of pi was only known to 35 decimal places (today it is to 1.2411 trillion!).

It took Leonardo Da Vinci 10 years to paint the Mona Lisa.

The atomic symbol for iron is Fe, after the original name for iron, which was Ferric.

The ancient Greeks first grew carrots as a form of medicine and not as a food.

In 1886 Coca Cola was introduced as an 'intellectual beverage' to boost brain power.

New Zealand was the first place in the world to allow women to vote.

The first US coast to coast aeroplane flight occurred in 1911, and took 49 days.

Before 1863, the postal service in the United States was free.

The first taxi service began in New York in 1907.

Pez was invented in 1927.

Before 1850, golf balls were made of leather and were stuffed with feathers.

The character Superman dates back to June 1938.

The Colgate toothpaste company started out making starch, soap, and candles.

Most dinosaurs lived to be more than 100 years old.

The first city to mint its own gold coins was Florence, Italy in 1252.

Women were not allowed to vote in France until 1944.

The world's first paved streets were laid in Rome in 170 B.C..

Dinosaurs lived on Earth for over 165 million years before they became extinct.

Jellyfish have been on Earth for over 650 million years.

Sharks have been on Earth for over 400 million years.

The game of Tug-of-war was an Olympic sport from 1900-1920.

Nintendo first produced playing cards.

England's Stonehenge is over 5,000 years old.

The first ground vacuum packed coffee was introduced in 1900.

The dollar was established as the official currency of the US in 1785.

In 1900 the average life span in the US was 47.

Flushable toilets were in use in ancient Rome.

The first ever credit card was a Diner's Club card issued in 1950.

The world's first roller coaster opened in 1884 at Coney Island, New York.

England's first great industry was wool.

Mapping is older than writing.

The corkscrew was invented in 1890.

The typewriter was invented in 1829.

The dishwasher was invented in 1889.

The wristwatch was invented in 1904.

The oldest cockroach fossils are over 280 million years old.

Geography and Travel

The barracuda fish is nicknamed the 'tiger of the sea'.

A barracuda's eyes are always open.

The Amazon rainforest produces more than 20% of the world's oxygen supply.

The Amazon River pushes so much water into the Atlantic Ocean that you can dip into fresh water in the ocean.

The volume of water in the Amazon river is greater than the next eight largest rivers in the world combined, and three times the flow of all rivers in the United States.

Antarctica is the only area of land on our planet that is not owned by any country.

Ninety percent of the world's ice covers Antarctica.

This ice also represents seventy percent of all the fresh water in the world.

Antarctica is essentially just a very cold desert.

Although covered with ice (all but 0.4% of it), Antarctica is the driest place on the planet, with an absolute humidity lower than the Gobi desert.

Brazil got its name from the nut, not the other way around.

Canada has more lakes than the rest of the world combined.

Next to Warsaw, Chicago has the largest Polish population in the world.

Woodward Avenue in Detroit, Michigan, carries the designation M-1, named so because it was the first paved road anywhere.

Damascus, Syria, was flourishing a couple of thousand years before Rome was founded in 753 BC, making it the oldest continuously inhabited city in existence.

Istanbul is the only city in the world located on two continents.

The term "The Big Apple" was coined by touring jazz musicians of the 1930's who used the slang expression "apple" for any town or city. So to play New York City is to play the big time - The Big Apple.

There are more Irish in New York City than in Dublin, Ireland.

There are more Italians in New York City than in Rome, Italy.

There are more Jews in New York City than in Tel Aviv, Israel.

There are no natural lakes in the state of Ohio, every single one is manmade.

The smallest island with country status is Pitcairn in Polynesia, at just 1.75 sq. miles/4,53 sq. km.

The first city to reach a population of 1 million people was Rome, Italy, in 133 B.C.

Siberia contains more than 25 per cent of the world's forests.

The smallest sovereign entity in the world is the Sovereign Military Order of Malta (S.M.O.M.). It is located in the city of Rome, Italy, has an area of two tennis courts, and as of 2001 has a population of 80, 20 less people than the Vatican.

Pakuri Arawak Territory in Guyana has a population of 1,300 and an area of 240 square miles.

In the Sahara Desert there is a town named Tidikelt, which did not receive a drop of rain for ten years.

The driest place on Earth is in the valleys of the Antarctic near Ross Island. There has been no rainfall there for two million years.

Spain (Espana) literally means 'the land of rabbits.'

The chance that a road is unpaved in the U.S.A. is 1 per cent, while in Canada it is 75 per cent.

The deepest hole ever made in the world is in Texas.

The Eisenhower interstate system requires that one-mile in every five must be straight. These straight sections are usable as airstrips in times of war or other emergencies.

The Kingdom of Tonga is the only monarchy in the Pacific.

The Trans-Siberian railway crosses exactly 3901 bridges.

The Philippines archipelago includes 7,107 islands.

The words "Allahu Akbar" are repeated 22 times on the flag of Iran.

The seven largest countries in the world (Russia, Canada, USA, China, Australia, Brazil and Argentina) cover half of the Earth's territory.

There are only the five states/countries In Europe that border only one other state – Portugal, Italy, San Marino, Vatican City and Monaco.

The Mexican volcano "Paricutin" eruption lasted for nine years (1943 to 1952). During this time the cone of the volcano grew to 2,774 meters.

London's equivalent of the New York Wall Street is known as Lombard Street.

The five boroughs of New York City are The Bronx, Brooklyn, Queens, Staten Island and Manhattan.

The largest desert in Europe – Ryn Sands - is located between the Volga and the Urals (in Kazakhstan and Russia).

Japan has more than 3,900 islands.

There are three places called Peru and nine called Paris in the U.S.

Less than one per cent of the Caribbean islands are inhabited.

Of the 25 highest peaks of the world, 19 are in the Himalayas.

It wasn't until the 1980's that Bhutan had a phone.

The coldest capital city of the world is Ulan Bator, the capital of Mongolia.

----

336 rivers empty into Lake Baikal, but it has only one that flows - Angara.

The last eruption of the Japanese volcano Mount Fuji occurred in 1707.

The largest ports in the world are Rotterdam, Singapore, Kobe, New York, New Orleans.

Nauru is the only state in the world that has no official capital.

Cuba is the only Caribbean island that has a railway.

The first capital of the Russian state was Ladoga.

There are the 17 active volcanoes in Japan.

On February 18, 1979 it actually snowed in the Sahara Desert.

In Thailand, it is considered impolite to use a fork while eating.

The center of Europe is located in Ukraine.

Several buildings in Manhattan have their own zip code.

The highest of the extinct volcanoes on Earth is Aconcagua, located in Argentina. Its reaches an altitude of 6,960 meters.

Montpelier (Vermont) is the smallest state capital in the U.S.. It has a population of about 9,000.

The state capital of Montpelier Vermont is the only state capital in the U.S. where there is no McDonald's.

One of the largest Icelandic geysers, located on the slopes of the volcano Hekla, is called... Geyser.

The national anthem of Greece has 158 versions.

The river Ob has 150,000 inflows.

There are no rivers in Saudi Arabia.

The Red Sea is the warmest sea in the world.

Local people of Lesbos island in Greece are named lesbosiyts lesbosianks instead but not lesbians.

The Chinese and Korean family name always comes first - before the given name.

The widest street in the world is located in Brasilia.

In the town of Calama, located in the Chilean Atacama Desert, it never rains.

The nation of Papua New Guinea consists of the islands of New Britain and New Ireland.

In South America, the only two countries that do not have access to the ocean are Bolivia and Paraguay.

Hong Kong has the highest number of Rolls-Royce cars per capita.

Lebanon is the only state in the Middle East, in which there is no desert.

Unlike most African nations, Ethiopia has been never a European colony.

In May 1948, two New Zealand volcanoes erupted simultaneously.

France, Italy and Chile once formally recognized the existence of UFOs.

The cleanest sea in the world is the Weddell Sea in Antarctica.

There are seven cities along the tourist route "Golden Ring of Russia".

We share 98.4% of our DNA with a chimp - and 70% with a slug.

97.2% of the Earth's water is salt water.

It takes the Earth exactly 365.242199 days to orbit the Sun - and that is why every four years we need a leap year.

The biggest known star has a diameter of 1800 million miles, making it 2000 times bigger than the Sun.

If emissions of carbon dioxide were halted today, it would take more than a century for the atmospheric level of carbon dioxide to approach its pre-industrial era level.

More types of fish swim in Brazil's Amazon River than in the entire Atlantic Ocean.

The 'Red Planet' isn't really red at all. NASA photographs indicate that it is more of a tan or butterscotch color.

The deepest lake in the world is Lake Baikal in the former USSR.

Sound travels 15 times faster through steel than through the air.

The increased electricity used by modern appliances is causing a shift in the Earth's magnetic field. By the year 2327, the North Pole will be located in mid-Kansas, while the South Pole will be just off the coast of East Africa.

The largest pearl ever found was 620 carats.

Time slows down near a black hole; inside it stops completely.

Quicksand is formed when sand, clay, and water are mixed in just the right way, with a surface that seems solid until you step on it, and then it suddenly becomes liquid.

In one year, the average tree gives off enough oxygen to allow four people to breathe for a year.

Our galaxy's oldest stars are Red Dwarfs, which are also the smallest and most abundant, constituting 70% of the galaxy's stars.

If you take one pound of cobwebs and spread them out in one straight line, it would go around the Earth twice.

If you attempted to count the stars in a galaxy at a rate of one every second it would take around 3,000 years to count them all.

When a jet plane reaches a speed of 1,000 km h (620 mph), the length of the plane becomes one atom shorter than its original length.

Earth's atmosphere is, proportionally, thinner than the skin of an apple.

The distance from the surface of Earth to the center is about 3,963 miles.

The fastest moon in our solar system circles Jupiter once every seven hours - traveling at 70,400 miles per hour.

About 400 billion gallons of water are used every day.

The largest pumpkin on record weighed 377 pounds.

To an observer standing on Pluto, the Sun would appear no brighter than Venus appears in our evening sky.

A bean's cell contains more DNA than a human cell does.

The planet Saturn has a density lower than water.

The Volcano Olympus Mons on Mars rises 16 miles (26 kilometers) into the Martian sky.

Blood is six times thicker than water.

In the Durango desert, in Mexico, there's a spot called the "Zone of Silence," where you can't pick up clear TV or radio signals.

Seventy per cent of all water used by humans worldwide is for irrigation.

Every human spent about half an hour as a single cell.

4,800 years ago the ancient Egyptians worked out that there were 365 days in a year.

A bucket filled with Earth would weigh about 5 time more than the same bucket filled with the substance of the Sun.

Uranus' orbital axis is tilted at 90 degrees.

Orchids are the largest family of flowering plants with approximately 35,000 species.

It takes a plastic container 50,000 years to start decomposing.

In deep space most lubricants will disappear.

If everyone in the U.S. recycled their Sunday newspaper, it would save 500,000 trees every week.

Traveling at the speed of 186,000 miles per second, light takes six hours to travel from Pluto to Earth.

There are parts of Europe, particularly in the south of France where it has rained red rain. Some scientists believe that they are caused by a reddish dust that is blown all the way from the Sahara Desert Others .

There are three golf balls sitting on the moon.

A modern chip of silicon a quarter-inch square has the capacity of the original 1949 ENIAC computer, which occupied a city block.

Broccoli has a nervous system.

The Hubble telescope is so powerful that it is like pointing a beam of light at a dime that is 200 miles away.

In the Bay of Fundy, located between New Brunswick and Nova Scotia in Canada, the tide sometimes rises 10 feet in one hour.

Sound at the right vibration level can bore holes through a solid object.

Tomatoes and cucumbers are fruits.

The clock at the National Bureau of Standards in Washington, D.C., will gain or lose only one second in 300 years because it uses cesium atoms that beat 300 billion times a second.

Traveling at the speed of light it would take a spaceship just 1.2822 seconds to reach the Moon.

Only one satellite has ever been destroyed by a meteor: the European Space Agency's Olympus in 1993.

By 2150 there will be 10 billion humans. In 2000 there were six billion.

The soft plastic headphones used on airplanes create a warm, moist environment in the ear canal that is ideal for breeding bacteria.

One tree can filter up to 27 kg of pollutants from the air each year.

A "fulgurite" is fossilized lightning. It forms when a powerful lightning bolt melts the soil into a glass-like state.

When a pickle is plugged into an electric current it turns yellow, and gives off an awful smell.

Compact discs (CD's) read from the inside to the outside edge, the reverse of how a record works.

A car traveling at a constant speed of 60 miles per hour would take over 48 million years to reach the nearest star, Proxima Centauri. This is about 685,000 average human lifetimes.

In St. John, New Brunswick, there is a Waterfall that flows upward.

A raisin dropped in a glass of fresh champagne will bounce up and down continuously from the bottom of the glass to the top.

A dripping water tap wastes an average of 40 kw hours of electricity per month. This is the equivalent of running a television eight hours a day for about 31 days.

The Andes Mountain range in South America is 4,525 miles long and is the world's longest.

There are five trillion trillion atoms in one pound of iron.

Sterling silver is not pure silver. Because pure silver is too soft to be used in most jewelry and other popular silver items, it is mixed with copper to give it strength.

The densest substance on Earth is the metal "osmium".

A cumulonimbus cloud can be enormous: six miles across and eleven miles high - and twice as high as Mount Everest.

Portland cement is used for underwater work. Unlike other concrete, it hardens because of a chemical reaction it has with the water, not because the water mixed with it evaporates.

60-65 million years ago dolphins and humans shared a common ancestor - the Mesonychid.

Trees get about 90% of their nutrition from the atmosphere, and only about 10% from the soil.

Vinegar was the strongest acid known in the ancient times.

All known vitamins are found in eggs except vitamin C.

A cosmic year is the amount of time it takes the sun to revolve around the center of the Milky Way, which is about 225 million years.

Microbial life can survive on the cooling rods of a nuclear reactor.

In winter the Antarctic ice covers 10% of our planet.

The Telegraph plant is a tropical plant usually found in Asia and the South Pacific. The plant has the ability to shake its leaves up and down on its own.

Ingredients in pineapples might cause an abortion if eaten during pregnancy.

Every day is about 55 billionths of a second longer than the day before it.

The averaged size tree can provide enough wood to make 170,000 pencils.

The Earth is not really round. Its shape is called an oblate spheroid, meaning it's slightly flattened on the top and bottom poles.

Bacteria, the tiniest free-living cells, are so small that a single drop of liquid contains as many as 50 million of them.

You are more likely to be struck by lightning than to be eaten by a shark.

You are more likely to be infected by flesh-eating bacteria than you are to be struck by lightning.

The liquid inside young coconuts can be used as a substitute for blood plasma.

A neutron star is 15 miles across and weighs more than the Sun.

A ball of glass will bounce higher than a ball of rubber, and a ball of solid steel will bounce higher than one made entirely of glass.

The temperature on the surface of Mercury exceeds 430 degrees C during the day, and, at night, plummets to minus 180 degrees C.

Salt is one of very few spices that is all taste, and no smell.

A scientist at Michigan State University has calculated that the production of a single hen egg requires about 120 gallons of water, a loaf of bread requires 300 gallons, and a pound of beef - 3,500 gallons.

A green flash is sometimes seen just as the sun sets or rises. This occurs because green light is bent most strongly out of the spectrum by the atmosphere.

Up to 15,000 dust mites can live and thrive in just one gram of dust.

A single cup of coffee contains over 1000 chemical substances.

A dog was killed by a meteor impact at Nakhla, Egypt, in 1911.

Bamboo trees fall under the group of woody perennial evergreen plants. It is the fastest growing woody plant in the world - at up to four feet each day.

Microorganisms have been brought back to life by researchers after being frozen in permafrost for three million years.

Our oldest radio broadcasts of the 1930s have already traveled past 100,000 stars.

There are more insects in just one square mile of fertile soil than there are human beings on the entire planet.

A bolt of lightning can strike the earth with a force as great as 100 million volts.

The footprints of astronauts who landed on the moon should last at least 10 million years, since the moon has no atmosphere.

Every drop of seawater contains approximately one billion gold atoms.

The total combined weight of the world's ant population is heavier than the weight of the human population.

Humans have 46 chromosomes, peas have 14 and crayfish have 200.

The first man-made item to exceed the speed of sound was the leather whip.

At over 2000 kilometers long the Great Barrier Reef off the north-east coast of Australia is the largest living structure on Earth.

Mosquitoes have been found to prefer biting people with smelly feet.

At present, even the most powerful computers cannot accurately process as many instructions as a goldfish brain can.

America produces 215 million tons of solid garbage every year.

The Earth gets heavier each day by several tons, as meteoric dust settles on it.

There are 62,000 miles of blood vessels in the human body - laid out, they would circle the Earth 2.5 times.

Butterflies taste with their hind feet and their taste sensation works on touch - this allows them to determine whether a leaf is edible.

The research spacecraft Helios B came within a record 27 million miles of the Sun.

----

314 acres of trees are used to make the newsprint for the average Sunday edition of the New York Times. This equates to nearly 63,000 trees.

Almost 10 people more live on this Earth now, than before you finished reading this, due to the birth rate.

A "lost world" exists in the Indonesian jungle that is home to dozens of unknown animal and plant species.

A thimbleful of a neutron star would weigh over 100 million tons.

There's enough energy in ten minutes of one hurricane to match the nuclear stockpiles of the world.

Although rainforests only cover 7% of the Earth's surface, at least 40% of all animal and plant species live in them.

The temperature at the centre of the Earth is estimated to be around 5,500 degrees Celsius.

All the Earth's oceans combined contain enough salt to cover all the continents to a depth of nearly 500 feet.

Variations in the color of pearls are still a mystery, but some experts believe that high water temperatures contribute to the differences.

The Himalayan goji berry contains, weight for weight, more iron than steak, more beta carotene than carrots and more vitamin C than oranges.

We can produce laser light a million times brighter than the Sun's light.

To escape the Earth's gravity, a rocket needs to travel at seven miles a second.

----

65 million years ago, the impact of an asteroid is estimated to have had the power of 10 million H-Bombs.

Windows 2000 operating system contained 29 million lines of code.

The deepest part of any ocean in the world is the Mariana trench in the Pacific with a depth of 35,797 feet.

The International Space Station orbits at 248 miles above the Earth.

Volcanoes on Io eject material at speeds of 3,500 kph.

Jupiter's moon, Europa, is completely covered in ice.

The interstellar gas cloud Sagittarius B contains a billion, billion, billion liters of alcohol.

If the world were tilted one degree more either way, the planet would not be habitable because the area around the equator would be too hot and the poles would be too cold.

Scientists have determined that fungi are more closely related to human beings and animals than to other plants.

Annually, enough energy is saved by recycling steel to supply Los Angeles with electricity for almost 10 years.

Wounds infested with maggots heal quickly and without spread of infection.

For every 10 successful attempts to climb Mount Everest there is one fatality.

According to experts, large caves actually "breathe". They inhale and exhale great quantities of air when the barometric pressure on the surface changes, and air rushes in or out seeking equilibrium.

A typical hurricane produces the energy equivalent of 8,000 one megaton bombs.

The Himalayas mountain range cover one-tenth of the Earth's surface.

The fastest spacecraft can go 40,000 mph.

Plant seeds that have been stored for more than 200 years can be brought back to life.

Sports

There are over 1300 football stadiums in the world.

To host the FIFA World Cup final, a stadium must have a minimum seating capacity of 40,000.

There are 294 stadiums in the world, which could host the FIFA final. "Rungrado May Day Stadium" in North Korea tops the list with a capacity of 150,000.

The highest scoring professional soccer game of all time was 149-0.

Football players run approximately 10 km during one game.

Tennis players run around 5km during a game.

In 1966, the World Cup trophy was stolen and later found by a dog days before the tournament began.

Early footballs began as animal bladders or stomachs that would easily fall apart if kicked too much.

With every World Cup there is a new official ball used for the tournament.

Soccer is called football in every country except the USA, Australia and Canada.

A league match between Sportivo Ameliano and General Caballero in Paraguay saw 20 Red cards.

The Romans played a game called harpastum which is said to be an ancestor of modern football.

There is a FIFA Women's World Cup.

Pele was the youngest player to score a hat-trick at a FIFA World Cup. He was 17 years old.

The Golden Ball Award is presented to the best player at each FIFA world cup finals.

Carlos Alberto Parreira is one of two managers who have coached five different teams at the FIFA World Cup.

Sir Alex Ferguson managed Manchester United from 1986 to 2013.

Derby means a sporting fixture between two teams from the same town, city or region.

The wave is an example of rhythm, when groups of spectators stand, yell and raise their hands.

English teacher, soldier and football referee, Ken Aston, developed yellow and red cards.

Penalties in football/soccer were first introduced in the 1890/91 season in England.

A 2005 Nike advertisement featuring Ronaldinho was the first YouTube video to break one million views.

The Battle for Bramall Lane is the informal name given to an English First Division.

Paul Gascoigne or Gazza is a former England international footballer.

Brazilians call soccer the Jogo Bonito.

Geoff Hurst is the only person who won a medal in football and cricket.

The record number of Football League goals scored in a single day is 209.

The first live coverage of a soccer match shown on television, was in 1937.

Gary Neville and Phil Neville on November 29 2006 became the first brothers to captain opposing teams.

Manchester City holds the record for the fastest century of goals scored during a Premier League season.

No English Manager has won an English Premier League.

Manchester United holds the record for most league titles.

The FA Cup is an annual cup competition in English football.

Since its formation in 1929, only eight football clubs have won the Spanish La Liga.

Oleg Salenko is the only player in World Cup history to have scored five goals in a single match.

Mexico holds the record for most defeats in World Cup history, losing 24 matches.

40% of all footballs are made in Sialkot, Pakistan.

Football nets were not introduced until the 1890s.

Guillermo Stabile scored a hat-trick during his international debut.

It takes 3000 cows to supply the NFL with enough leather for a year's supply of footballs.

----

300 million golf balls are lost in the United States alone, every year.

Babe Ruth wore cabbage leaf under his cap to keep him cool.
He changed it every two innings.

Kresimir Cosic is only non-American player in the NBA Hall of
Fame.

Pittsburgh is the only city where all major sports teams have the
same black and gold colors.

Diddle for the middle is the slang expression for the start of a
darts game.

The fastest round of golf by a team was 9 minutes and 28
seconds.

Fishing is the biggest participant sports in the world.

Football (soccer) is the most attended and watched (on TV) sport
in the world.

The first AFL/NFL championship to be called a "Super Bowl" was Super Bowl III; on January 12, 1969.

The Dallas Cowboys and the Pittsburgh Steelers have had the most Super Bowl appearances at eight each.

The Pittsburgh Steelers have won the most Super Bowl titles – six championships. The Dallas Cowboys and San Francisco 49ers have each won five times.

Boxing became a legal sport in 1901.

More than 100 million people hold hunting licenses.

In 1975, Junko Tabei from Japan became the first woman to reach the top of Everest.

The record for the most major league baseball career innings is held by Cy Young, with 7,356 innings.

The Major League Baseball teams use about 850,000 balls per season. Padded batting gloves have helped many of these balls leave the stadium due to home runs.

In 1898, one of the first programs to be broadcasted on radio was a yacht race that took place in British waters.

Sports command the biggest television audiences, led by the summer Olympics, World Cup Football and Formula One racing.

Gymnasiums were introduced in 900 BC and Greek athletes practiced in the nude to the accompaniment of music. They also performed naked at the Olympic Games.

The very first Olympic race, held in 776 BC, was won by Coroebus, a chef.

The first modern Olympic Games were held in Athens, Greece in 1896. There were 311 male, but no female, competitors.

In his time, Michael Schumacher was the highest paid sportsman, ahead of Tiger Woods and Arnold Palmer. (Not including sponsorship endorsements.)

The high jump method of jumping head first and landing on the back is called the Fosbury Flop.

About 42,000 tennis balls are used in the approximately 650 matches in the Wimbledon Championship.

The longest tennis match took place at Wimbledon 2010 when John Isner of the United States beat Nicolas Mahut of France, in a match that lasted 11 hours and 5 minutes, played over 3 days.

A baseball ball has exactly 108 stitches, a cricket ball has between 65 and 70 stitches.

A soccer ball is made up of 32 leather panels, held together by 642 stitches.

Basketball and rugby balls are made from synthetic material. Earlier, pigs' bladders were used as rugby balls.

The baseball home plate is 17 inches wide.

The very first motor car land speed record was set by Ferdinand Verbiest.

The record for the most NASCAR wins is held by Richard Petty: 200 wins (and seven championships).

Sébastien Loeb won the World Rally Championship a record nine times, taking the title every year between 2004 and 2012.

Golf is the only sport ever played on the moon – on 6 February 1971 astronaut Alan Shepard hit a golf ball.

The Romans played a game resembling golf, using a stick to hit a feather-stuffed ball.

The word GOLF is not the abbreviation for "Gentlemen Only, Ladies Forbidden." It derives from an old German word "kolb," meaning club.

Bill Klem served the most seasons as a Major League umpire – 37 years, starting in 1905.
The oldest continuous trophy in sports is the America's Cup. It started in 1851, with Americans winning for a straight 132 years until Australia took the Cup in 1983.

Volleyball was invented by William George Morgan of Holyoke, Massachusetts in 1895.

A badminton shuttle easily travels at 180 kph (112 mph).

Ferenc Szisz from Romania, driving a Renault, won the first Formula One Grand Prix held at Le Mans, France in 1906.

Stéphane Peterhansel holds the record for most Dakar Rally wins; he won the motorcycle category (on a Yamaha) six times and has won the car category five times.

Competing in three Olympics, between 1956 and 1964, Soviet gymnast Larissa Latynina won 18 medals (9 gold, 5 silver and 4 bronze). She held the record for most Olympic medals for 48 years until surpassed by American swimmer Michael Phelps; from 2004 until 2012 he won 22 medals.

A tennis court is 23.8 m long and 11 m wide for doubles matches, and 23.8 m long and 8.2 m wide for singles matches.

The height of a tennis net is 0.9 m.

The tennis term love is derived from l'oeuf, the French word for egg, symbolizing zero.

In 1986 yellow balls were used at Wimbledon for the first time to make them visible for the TV cameras.

Tennis was an Olympic event from 1896 to 1924 and was reintroduced into the games in 1988.

In 1900 Dwight Davis gave his name to a competition between the United states and Great Britain. More than 60 countries now compete for the Davis cup annually.

The four tournaments that make up the Tennis Grand Slam are Wimbledon, the US Open, the Australian Open and the French Open.

The tennis term deuce derives from deux, the French word for two, meaning that an advantage of two points must be gained to win the the game.

Catgut, used in the making of tennis racket strings, is made out of the intestines of various animals (but not cats!).

A tennis tiebreaker comes into operation when the set score is six games all.

In 1877 British tennis player Spencer Gore was the first ever winner of the Wimbledon trophy beating fellow British player William Marshall.

125,000 golf balls a year are hit into the water at the famous 17th hole of the Stadium Course at Sawgrass.

The longest drive in golf ever is 515 yards. The longest putt was 375 feet.

Golfer, Phil Mickelson, who plays left-handed, is actually right handed.

The chances of making two holes-in-one in a round of golf are one in 67 million.

Tiger Woods snagged his first ace at the tender age of eight years old.

Balls travel significantly further on hot days.

The longest golf course in the world is the par 77 International Golf Club in Massachusetts which measures in at 8325 yards.

The highest golf course in the world is the Tactu Golf Club in Morococha, Peru, which sits 14,335 feet above sea level at its lowest point.

The longest golf hole in the world is the 7th hole (par 7) of the Sano Course at the Satsuki Golf Club in Japan. It measures an in at 909 m.

The largest bunker in the world is Hell's Half Acre on the 585-yard 7th hole of the Pine Valley Course in New Jersey.

The driver swing speed of an average lady golfer is 62mph; 96 mph for an average LPGA professional; 84mph for an average male golfer; 108 mph for an average PGA Tour player; 130mph for Tiger Woods; 148-152 mph for a national long drive champion.

The youngest golfer to shoot a hole-in-one was Coby Orr, who was five years old at the time. It happened in Littleton, Colorado, in 1975.

22.8% of golfers are women.

Golf was banned in Scotland from 1457 to 1502 to ensure citizens wouldn't waste time when preparing for an English invasion.

The term birdie comes from an American named Ab Smith. While playing in 1899, he played what he described as a "bird of a shot", which became "birdie" over time.

80% of all golfers will never achieve a handicap of less than 18.

The Houston Astrodome was the first baseball stadium to have a roof over its playing field.

A golf course within 6.5 km of the coast is called a links.

The largest football stadium in the world is the Maracana in Rio de Janeiro, Brazil, which hosted the 1950 World Cup Final in front of a crowd of 199,854. Today the crowd capacity is limited to 80,000, as parts of the stadium are deemed to be unsafe.

In 1931 tennis star Lili de Alvarez became the first-ever woman to wear a pair of shorts at Wimbledon.

Only 13 nations contested the first football world cup in 1930, which saw Uruguay winning the trophy.

The first ever footballer to win 100 caps for England was the Wolves defender Billy Wright.

Roger Bannister ran the first ever under four minute mile in 1954 at an Oxford running track: the time was 3 minutes, 59.4 seconds.

The first foreign footballing nation to defeat England at Wembley was Hungary.

The first English Football League team to install an artificial pitch was the Queens Park Rangers in 1981.

Olympic gold medals are actually made mostly of silver.

Dimples on a golf ball help reduce drag, allowing the ball to fly further than a ball without dimples.

Anaerobic exercise refers to high intensity activities over a short duration (e.g. sprinting) while aerobic exercise refers to physical activity performed at a moderate level over longer periods of time (e.g. jogging).

Regular exercise helps boost the immune system.

The string tension of most tennis racquets is around 50 to 70 pounds. With lower tension, a tennis racquet produces less control and more power while higher tension produces more control and less power.

The official distance of a marathon is 42.195 kilometres (26.219 miles).

The tallest basketball players to ever play in the NBA were Manute Bol (from Sudan) and Gheorghe Muresan (from Romania). They were both 7 ft 7 in tall (231 cm).

The fastest recorded tennis serves are over 155 mph (250 kph).

Snowboarders and ice skaters glide on a thin layer of water as their skates and boards heat the snow beneath them.

Modern swimwear has developed to the point where the fabric and designs are actually faster through the water than human skin. Controversial neck to ankle suits have been one of the reasons behind the consistent breaking of world record times since they were introduced around the year 2000.

Curling stones used in the Olympic sport of curling are made from granite.

The diameter of a full sized basketball is half the diameter of a basketball hoop.

CPSIA information can be obtained
at www.ICGtesting.com
Printed in the USA
LVOW01s1005180916

505125LV00016B/962/P